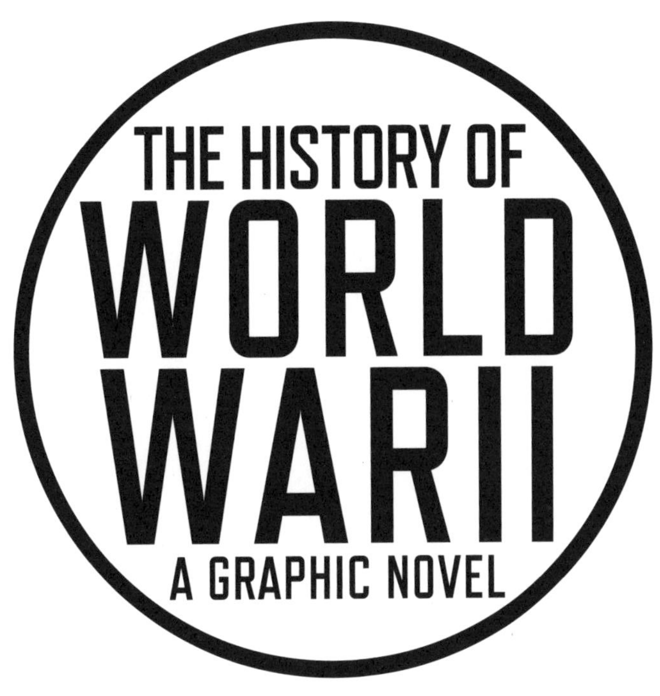

ILLUSTRATIONS BY
VICENTE CIFUENTES

STORY BY
ARNAUD DE LA CROIX

ABRAMS COMICARTS • NEW YORK

TABLE OF CONTENTS

INTRODUCTION

On November 11, 1918, at 11:11 a.m., as an armistice takes effect and Germany acknowledges its defeat before the Allied powers (Great Britain, France, and their allies, including Italy and the United States), Europe emerges from a slaughter of historic proportions.

Science and its many applications led to more industrialized methods of waging war, and the result is a bloodbath: more than eighteen million dead, nearly nine million of whom are civilians. The age of enlightenment and its notions that scientific rationality will ensure progress and happiness for humanity is seriously challenged.

The treaty signed at Versailles on June 28, 1919, holds Germany responsible for the first "world" conflict and forces the country to pay heavy reparations. We now think it more likely that during the summer of 1914, European nations were sleepwalking toward the irreversible, to use the words of historian Christopher Clark. More fundamentally, tensions between Great Britain—a maritime power at the head of an unrivaled colonial empire—and a Germany in the midst of an industrial and military boom at the center of Europe provided the breeding ground for violent outbreak.

In 1919, in Munich, a young Austrian-born corporal who fought on the Flanders front under the German flag refuses to demobilize. His name is Adolf Hitler, and he is thirty years old. After the war, the army is his only family, and his superiors recognize his talent as an orator. They provide him with some quick political training and use him as a trusted figure to counter the spread of communist ideologies within the barracks. He joins a small, far-right group in September and soon assumes leadership of it. Hitler rants in the beer halls against the "November criminals"—the politicians who signed the armistice. However, the leaders of the young republic founded in Weimar will not remain idle for long, as we shall see...

CHAPTER

1

A PACIFIED EUROPE?

1921–1925

BERLIN, LATE 1921.
WE ARE ABOUT TO ENTER ONE OF THE MOST SECRET PLACES IN THE GERMAN CAPITAL...

"GENTLEMEN" GATHER HERE, AWAY FROM PRYING EYES...

WITHIN THESE WALLS, GREAT BANKERS, POWERFUL LANDOWNERS, INDUSTRIALISTS, AND POLITICAL LEADERS DISCUSS THE FUTURE OF THE COUNTRY...

WE'VE BEEN WAITING FOR YOU!

MEINE HERREN, I'VE COME TO SHARE AN IDEA WITH YOU... ABOUT HOW TO BUILD UP OUR ARMY DESPITE THE RESTRICTIONS IMPOSED BY THE TREATY OF VERSAILLES.

GENTLEMEN, LENIN WAS OUR SECRET WEAPON DURING THE GREAT WAR...
EXACTLY. BY SENDING THAT AGITATOR FROM SWITZERLAND OVER TO RUSSIA, WE ENABLED THE BOLSHEVIK COUP, AND THE NEW RUSSIAN GOVERNMENT IMMEDIATELY SIGNED A PEACE AGREEMENT WITH GERMANY.

ON THE EASTERN FRONT, WE CARRIED THE DAY...
IT WAS THE JEWS' AND PROFITEERS' FAULT WE LOST THE WAR IN THE WEST BY BETRAYING THE NATION ON THE HOME FRONT!

HMM...THAT'S THE STAB-IN-THE-BACK THEORY, A MYTH SPREAD BY GENERAL LUDENDORFF. THE TRUTH IS THAT HE AND MARSHAL HINDENBURG FAILED IN THEIR WESTERN OFFENSIVE...
NO MATTER, GENTLEMEN! WHAT WE NEED NOW IS TO REBUILD THE HEER, THE GERMAN ARMY!
BUT HOW?

BY USING OUR "SECRET WEAPON" AGAIN: JOINING FORCES WITH... COMMUNIST RUSSIA!

WHAT? ALIGN OURSELVES WITH THE BOLSHEVIKS, WHO TRIED TO STIR UP A REVOLUTION IN GERMANY?!

IT'S NOT SUCH A STUPID IDEA... FRANCE, ENGLAND, AND THE UNITED STATES WANT TO PLAY GERMANY AND RUSSIA AGAINST EACH OTHER.
WE COULD COME TO A SECRET UNDERSTANDING!

SO BE IT!

ON APRIL 22, 1922, DURING THE GENOA CONFERENCE IN ITALY CALLED BY THE ALLIES, THE GERMANS AND RUSSIANS MEET IN RAPALLO 17 MILES AWAY...

GERMAN MINISTER RATHENAU AND SOVIET DIPLOMAT CHICHERIN SIGN A TRADE AGREEMENT THAT ALSO PUTS AN END TO THE PAYMENT OF REPARATIONS BETWEEN THEIR COUNTRIES.

THE FOLLOWING YEAR, ON NOVEMBER 9, HITLER, WITH THE HELP OF GENERAL LUDENDORFF, ATTEMPTS TO SEIZE POWER IN MUNICH.

WATCH OUT! THE POLICE ARE WAITING FOR US!

THEY WOULDN'T DARE SHOOT ME—WHY, I WAS THE STRATEGIST OF THE GREAT WAR!

DURING THE TRIAL FOLLOWING THE FAILED COUP, LUDENDORFF IS ACQUITTED, WHILE HITLER TURNS THE COURT INTO A POLITICAL PLATFORM...

SIXTEEN BRAVE GERMAN MEN HAVE FALLEN FOR THEIR COUNTRY! THE COURT OF HISTORY WILL BE THE JUDGE!

THE AGITATOR IS SENTENCED TO FIVE YEARS IN PRISON, BUT NOW ALL OF GERMANY KNOWS WHO HE IS.

THE LEADER OF THE NAZI PARTY IS RELEASED AFTER JUST NINE MONTHS....

I USED MY TIME IN THE SHADOWS TO WRITE MY BOOK, *MEIN KAMPF*.

IN THE FALL OF 1922, BENITO MUSSOLINI COMES TO POWER IN ITALY. ORIGINALLY A SOCIALIST, HE CREATES HIS OWN PARTY, THE FASCI DI COMBATTIMENTO—HENCE THE TERM "FASCIST." HE GATHERS FORMER VETERANS OF THE GREAT WAR, ESPOUSING THE IDEA THAT THEIR COUNTRY WAS BETRAYED AFTER JOINING THE ALLIES. THE FASCISTS MARCH ON ROME, AND THE KING OF ITALY APPOINTS THEIR LEADER AS HEAD OF THE GOVERNMENT.

INITIALLY, THE DICTATOR COOPERATES WITH ENGLAND AND FRANCE. IN 1925...

IN NEUTRAL SWITZERLAND, EUROPEAN LEADERS ARRANGE TO MEET IN OCTOBER ON THE SHORES OF LAKE MAGGIORE AT LOCARNO...

GENTLEMEN, I BELIEVE WE CAN REACH AN AGREEMENT...

INDEED, WE CAN.

FROM LEFT TO RIGHT, GERMANY'S GUSTAV STRESEMANN, ENGLAND'S NEVILLE CHAMBERLAIN, AND FRENCH LEADER ARISTIDE BRIAND...
JAWOHL, MEINE HERREN!

A NEW, PEACEFUL EUROPE SHALL RISE!

SIGNED BY FRANCE, THE UNITED KINGDOM, GERMANY, ITALY, BELGIUM, POLAND, AND CZECHOSLOVAKIA ON OCTOBER 16, 1925, THE LOCARNO TREATIES GUARANTEE GERMANY'S WESTERN BORDERS WITH THE INTENT TO ALLOW THE COUNTRY TO JOIN THE LEAGUE OF NATIONS.

Hitler and Ludendorff's failed coup on November 8 and 9, 1923, at the time seems like a minor incident in the history of the fledgling German republic, borne out of the ruins of the Great War. Hitler, however, decides he will come to power by legal means.

It takes him ten years... Initially, the Nazi Party—while known for its leader's fervent speeches and the violent actions of its militia (the Storm Troopers, or the SA)—achieves weak results in the elections: 3 percent of votes in 1924, 2.6 percent in 1928. At home, Germany is headed for economic recovery, and internationally, the country is on a path toward peaceful relations through the Locarno Treaties.

However, the collapse of the American stock market in 1929—the "Wall Street Crash"—changes everything. The shockwave from this financial crisis soon reaches Europe, hitting Germany hard in the early 1930s. Widespread unemployment results, and Germans, disillusioned with the impotency of the center-left and center-right parties, turn to the Nazi Party and, to a lesser extent, the Communist Party. Hitler temporarily tones down his virulent anti-Semitism and garners more than 37.3 percent of the vote in 1932.

In January 1933, on the advice of the centrist Franz von Papen, aging President Hindenburg agrees to let Hitler become the new German chancellor. Very quickly, the Nazis establish their dictatorship in Germany. Meanwhile, new tensions are emerging in the Far East...

CHAPTER

2

JAPAN TAKES ACTION

1931–1939

SEPTEMBER 18, 1931, 10:19 P.M., IN CHINA, SOUTHERN MANCHURIA.
IN MUKDEN, NEAR LAKE LIUTIAO, EVERYTHING IS CALM.

THEN, AT 10:20 P.M....

BOOOOOMMM

THE JAPANESE ARMY STATIONED IN THE KWANTUNG AREA OF MANCHURIA IS SOON ON HIGH ALERT.
I UNDERSTAND THAT THE JAPANESE RAILWAY IN MANCHURIA HAS BEEN SABOTAGED...
THIS ATTACK IS OUTRAGEOUS! WE MUST TAKE IMMEDIATE ACTION.

GENERAL ISHIWARA, DON'T WE NEED TO REPORT THIS TO TOKYO?

IF THIS FOOL KNEW THAT I WAS THE ONE WHO PLANTED THE BOMB.

HMM... IT'S POINTLESS. JAPANESE INTERESTS HAVE BEEN COMPROMISED. WE MUST REACT, AND QUICKLY!

ON SEPTEMBER 19, JAPANESE TROOPS INVADE MANCHURIA.

IN TOKYO, THE PRIME MINISTER IS GRANTED AN AUDIENCE WITH EMPEROR HIROHITO.

YOUR MAJESTY, I HAVE ORDERED THE KWANTUNG ARMY TO RETURN TO ITS GARRISONS.

GOOD.

BUT THE INVASION OF MANCHURIA CONTINUES. THE CHINESE RESISTANCE IS CRUSHED, AND NATIONALIST LEADER CHIANG KAI-SHEK IS OUSTED FROM THE PRESIDENCY, WEAKENING THE CHINESE NATIONALISTS AGAINST THE COMMUNISTS.

IN FEBRUARY 1932, A PUPPET GOVERNMENT SERVING JAPAN IS ESTABLISHED IN MANCHURIA, WITH TOKYO'S APPROVAL.
THE DEPOSED CHINESE EMPEROR PUYI IS PUT IN PLACE BY THE JAPANESE AS HEAD OF THE NEW STATE, MANCHUKUO.

FOR SOME TIME, THESE EVENTS CAPTIVATE WESTERN MEDIA.
CHINESE PRISONERS IN LATE 1931

IN BRUSSELS, YOUNG CARTOONIST GEORGES REMI, KNOWN AS HERGÉ, INCORPORATES THE MUKDEN INCIDENT INTO TINTIN'S ADVENTURE *THE BLUE LOTUS*.

IT WAS THE JAPANESE WHO DID IT!
THE JAPANESE EMBASSY IN BRUSSELS EXPRESSES ITS DISAPPROVAL.

ON FEBRUARY 25, 1933, IN GENEVA, IN NEUTRAL SWITZERLAND, WHERE THE LEAGUE OF NATIONS IS HEADQUARTERED...

WHO IS THAT MAN DRESSED IN MANCHURIAN ATTIRE?

THAT'S GENERAL ISHIWARA, WITH THE JAPANESE DELEGATION.

WITH JAPAN OCCUPYING MANCHURIA, HE'S TRYING TO TAUNT US...

CHINA IS IN CHAOS, WHICH IS WHY JAPAN HAS TO MAINTAIN ORDER WITH ITS NEARBY NEIGHBOR. THERE'S NO LONGER A GOVERNMENT IN CHINA WORTHY OF THE NAME, AND THE COUNTRY IS IN RUINS. WE'VE BEEN VERY PATIENT, BUT OUR PATIENCE IS WEARING THIN!

WE WILL NOW READ THE REPORT FROM THE LYTTON COMMISSION, A GROUP MADE UP OF INDEPENDENT EXPERTS WHO SPENT SIX WEEKS INVESTIGATING THE EVENTS IN MANCHURIA.

TO BEGIN WITH, IT APPEARS JAPANESE GRIEVANCES ARE PARTIALLY JUSTIFIED: JAPAN'S ECONOMIC INTERESTS IN CHINA HAVE NOT BEEN FULLY RESPECTED...

HOWEVER, THE JAPANESE CLEARLY HAD A METICULOUSLY PREPARED ATTACK PLAN, WHICH WAS CARRIED OUT ON THE NIGHT OF SEPTEMBER 18-19, 1931.

THIS WAS NOT AN ACT OF SELF-DEFENSE.

IT'S COMPLETE ANARCHY IN CHINA.

THE DOOR SLAMS SHUT, AND ON FEBRUARY 25, 1933, JAPAN WITHDRAWS FROM THE LEAGUE OF NATIONS, FORMALLY EXITING THE ORGANIZATION ON MARCH 27.

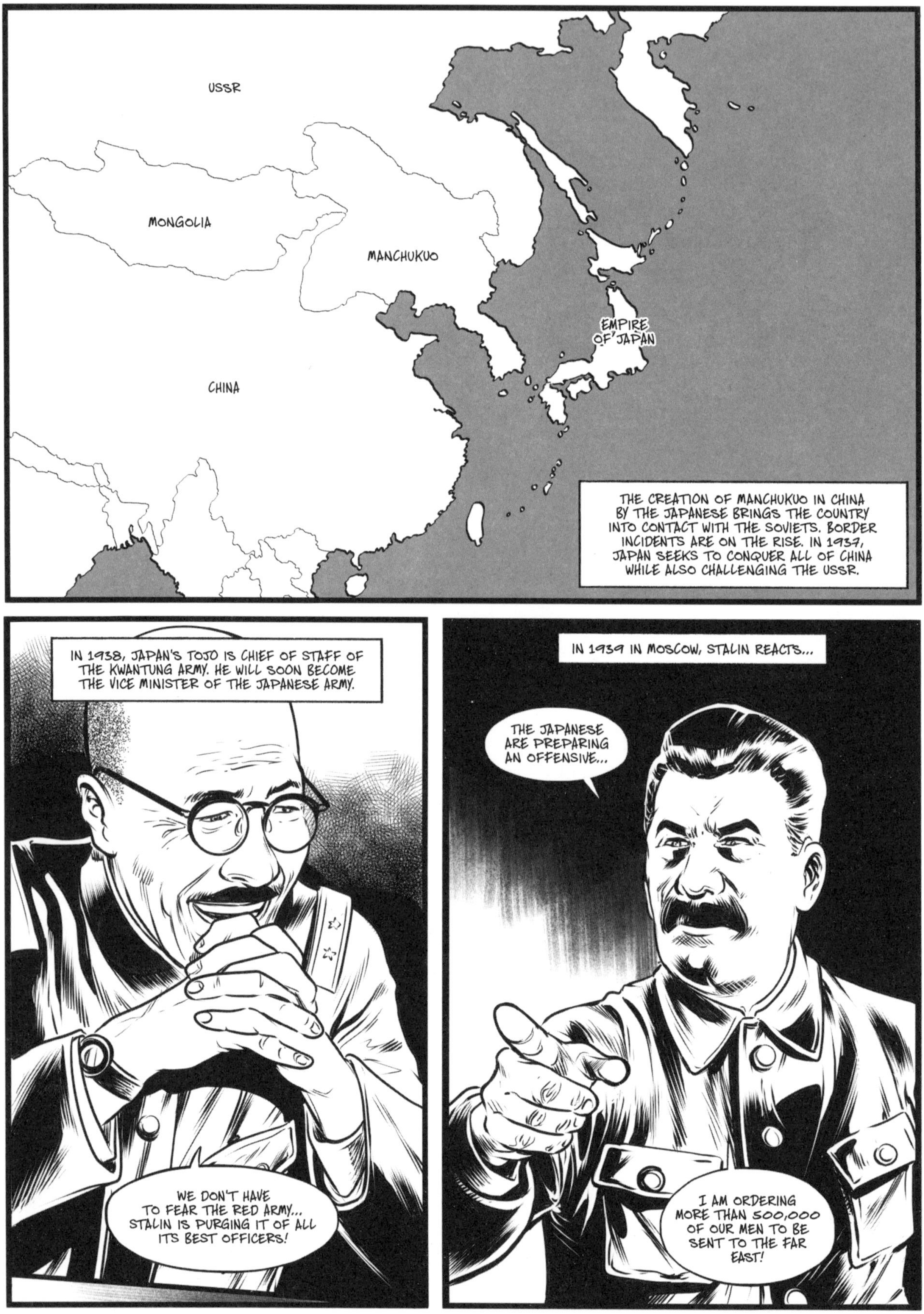

USSR

MONGOLIA

MANCHUKUO

EMPIRE OF JAPAN

CHINA

THE CREATION OF MANCHUKUO IN CHINA BY THE JAPANESE BRINGS THE COUNTRY INTO CONTACT WITH THE SOVIETS. BORDER INCIDENTS ARE ON THE RISE. IN 1937, JAPAN SEEKS TO CONQUER ALL OF CHINA WHILE ALSO CHALLENGING THE USSR.

ON MAY 4, NEAR THE MONGOLIAN BORDER, AN INCIDENT OCCURS INVOLVING MONGOLIAN HORSEMEN AND JAPANESE PATROL OFFICERS.

ON MAY 15, JAPANESE PLANES ENTER MONGOLIAN TERRITORY.

IN MOSCOW, STALIN URGENTLY SUMMONS HIS MINISTER OF WAR, VOROSHILOV.
THE KWANTUNG ARMY IS MOVING IN ON MONGOLIA, AND WE COMMITTED THREE YEARS AGO TO DEFEND THE MONGOLS.
IF MONGOLIA FALLS INTO THE HANDS OF THE JAPANESE, SIBERIA AND THE TRANS-SIBERIAN RAILWAY WILL BE IN GRAVE DANGER!

WE MUST DEAL A HARD BLOW TO THE JAPANESE! DISCOURAGE THEM ONCE AND FOR ALL FROM ADVANCING NORTHWARD. ESPECIALLY NOW THAT WE KNOW WAR IS BREWING IN EUROPE.

I'VE GOT THE RIGHT MAN FOR THE JOB.

*DIVISIONAL COMMANDER.

IN THE WEEKS THAT FOLLOW, THE TWO SIDES CONFRONT ONE ANOTHER ON LAND IN VIOLENT COMBAT.

THE JAPANESE ATTACK ON THE NIGHT OF JULY 2, BUT ARE GRADUALLY STAVED OFF. IN LATE AUGUST, THE RUSSIANS LAUNCH A COUNTERATTACK UNDER THE COMMAND OF ZHUKOV, WHO SENDS HIS RESERVES INTO BATTLE.

THE JAPANESE FORCES ARE SURROUNDED, AND FROM AUGUST 24 TO 31, THEY ARE BOMBARDED. THE KWANGTUNG ARMY IS CRUSHED AND HUMILIATED. JAPANESE DEATHS NUMBER 8,629, AND 3,000 ARE TAKEN PRISONER.

Is General Ishiwara, the man behind the 1931 Mukden incident and the Manchurian invasion, really the one who "started the war," as his biographer Bruno Birolli claims? He certainly embodies the belligerent mindset that characterizes many Japanese officers at the time, a mentality that would lead to the militarization of Japanese society throughout the 1930s, and to the Fifteen Year War (1931–1945), where Japan would face Chinese resistance until 1945, attack Dutch and French colonies in Southeast Asia from December 1941 to March 1945, and fight the United States in the Pacific starting in December 1941. This war does indeed begin at Mukden.

In their continued attempt to invade China, the Japanese capture Shanghai in 1937, and later attempt to move in on Outer Mongolia in 1939. It is a miscalculation, as we now know, and from that point on, they refrain from challenging the Soviet giant.

In addition, Zhukov makes a name for himself for the first time ever during the little-known battle of Khalkhin Gol. He is forty-three years old, but his career is far from over...

In the meantime, what's happening on the European continent?

CHAPTER

3

HITLER PUTS THE PRESSURE ON

1936–1938

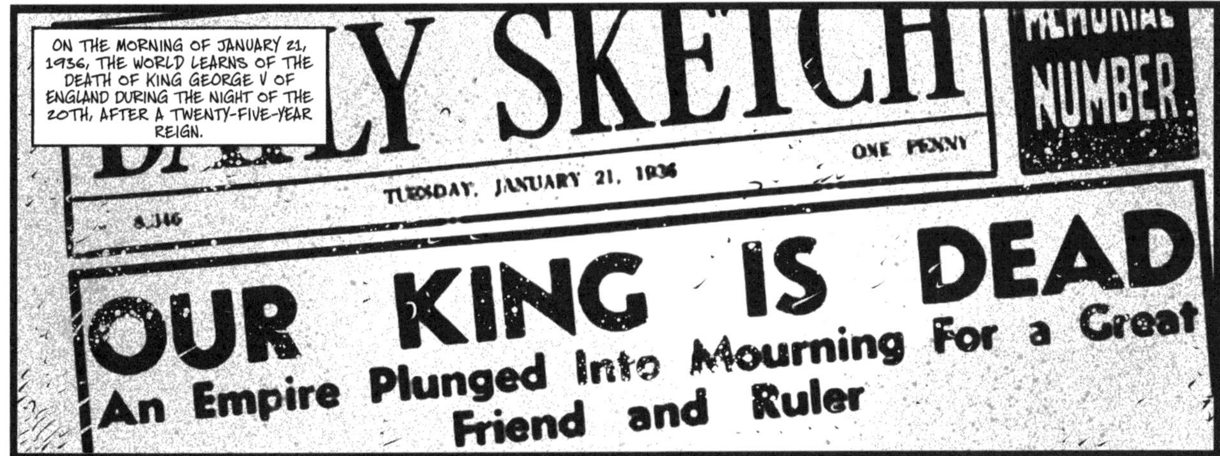
ON THE MORNING OF JANUARY 21, 1936, THE WORLD LEARNS OF THE DEATH OF KING GEORGE V OF ENGLAND DURING THE NIGHT OF THE 20TH, AFTER A TWENTY-FIVE-YEAR REIGN.
DAILY SKETCH
MEMORIAL NUMBER
ONE PENNY
TUESDAY, JANUARY 21, 1936
OUR KING IS DEAD
An Empire Plunged Into Mourning For a Great Friend and Ruler

IN BERLIN...
MEIN FÜHRER, A TELEGRAM FROM THE REICH AMBASSADOR IN WASHINGTON.
LET ME HAVE THAT.

HMM... OUR MAN HAS LEARNED FROM A RELIABLE SOURCE THAT THE NEW KING OF ENGLAND, EDWARD VIII, DISAPPROVES OF THE AGREEMENT BETWEEN HIS COUNTRY AND FRANCE, AND THAT HE...

SUPPOSEDLY HARBORS A GOOD DEAL OF SYMPATHY FOR THE DIFFICULT SITUATION GERMANY IS FACING.

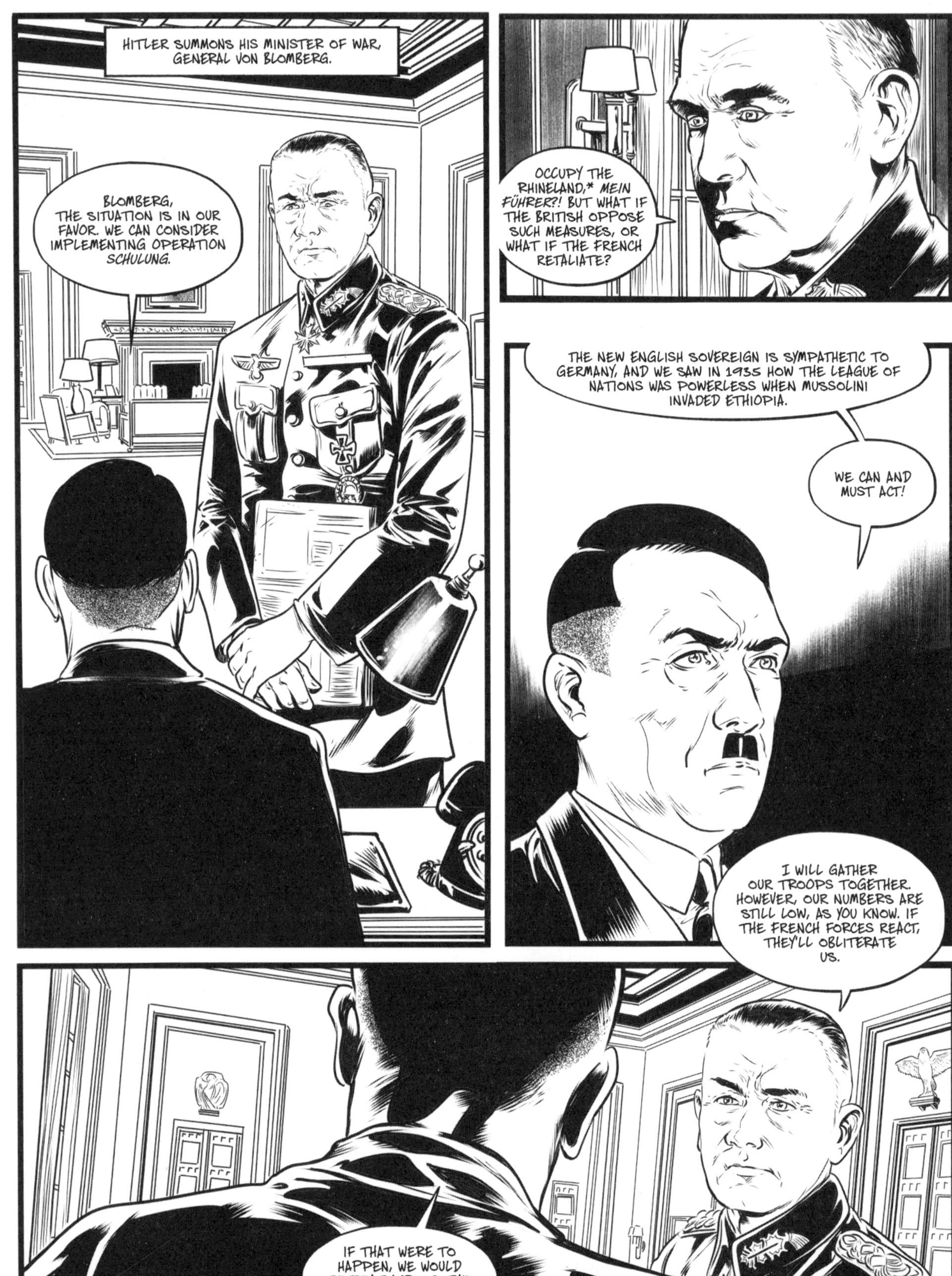

*DEMILITARIZATION OF THE REGION WAS IMPOSED ON GERMANY BY THE TREATY OF VERSAILLES TO CREATE A BUFFER ZONE WITH FRANCE.

JUST OVER A MONTH LATER, ON MARCH 7, GERMAN TROOPS ENTER THE RHINELAND.

THAT EVENING, HITLER TRAVELS TO MUNICH ON HIS SPECIAL TRAIN, ACCOMPANIED BY HIS ARCHITECT AND CONFIDANT ALBERT SPEER.

I'M WAITING FOR NEWS, SPEER.

IF THE ENGLISH MAKE ANY MOVE, THE FRENCH WILL INTERVENE.

THE KING OF ENGLAND WON'T INTERVENE. HE HAS KEPT HIS PROMISE. I'M RELIEVED...

*SEE CHAPTER 1.

THE VERY NEXT DAY, HITLER SUMMONS GÖRING AND VON BLOMBERG.

FRANCO, IN SPAIN, HAS REBELLED AGAINST THE SOCIALIST-COMMUNIST GOVERNMENT OF THE FRENTE POPULAR.*

IT'S A CIVIL WAR, AND HE'S ASKING US FOR HELP—FOR PLANES IN PARTICULAR!

*THE "POPULAR FRONT" IS A LEFT-WING ELECTORAL ALLIANCE FORMED IN SPAIN IN JANUARY 1936.
**THE AIR FORCE, WITH GÖRING APPOINTED AS ITS CHIEF.

*THE COMINTERN IS A COMMUNIST INTERNATIONAL ORGANIZATION LED BY THE USSR.
**THE UNION.
***"THE LEADER"; NAME GIVEN TO MUSSOLINI.

*WE KNOW WHAT WAS SAID THANKS TO NOTES TAKEN BY COLONEL HOSSBACH, WHO WAS ALSO PRESENT.

ON MARCH 12, 1938, THE GERMAN ARMY ENTERS AUSTRIA. THE AUSTRIAN ARMY DOES NOT PUT UP A FIGHT, AND THE LOCAL POPULATION WELCOMES THE GERMANS.
FRANCE AND ENGLAND DO NOT REACT.

LATE SEPTEMBER...
AMERICAN PRESIDENT WILSON, AT THE END OF THE GREAT WAR, ASSERTED THE RIGHT OF PEOPLES TO SELF-DETERMINATION.
IT'S TIME FOR THE GERMAN-SPEAKING SUDETEN REGIONS IN CZECHOSLOVAKIA TO JOIN GERMANY!

ONE BLOOD MEANS ONE REICH! AFTER THIS, I SOLEMNLY DECLARE, GERMANY SHALL HAVE NO FURTHER TERRITORIAL CLAIMS, AND EUROPE WILL BE AT PEACE FOR A THOUSAND YEARS.

LONDON AND PARIS HAD PLEDGED TO UPHOLD THE TERRITORIAL INTEGRITY OF CZECHOSLOVAKIA, AND NEVILLE CHAMBERLAIN, HEAD OF THE BRITISH GOVERNMENT, IS IN A TOUGH SPOT.
GENTLEMEN, HITLER HAS ISSUED AN ULTIMATUM, WHICH EXPIRES ON SEPTEMBER 28.
AND THE CZECHS ARE MOBILIZING THEIR TROOPS.
SO, IT'S WAR?

I'LL CALL ON MUSSOLINI!

IN ROME...
VERY WELL, I'LL PROPOSE A MEETING TO THE FÜHRER AS A LAST RESORT.

IN MUNICH, ON SEPTEMBER 30, 1938, A COMPROMISE IS SIGNED BY MUSSOLINI, HITLER, CHAMBERLAIN, AND FRANCE'S REPRESENTATIVE, DALADIER.
WE'VE AVOIDED A MAJOR CONFLICT.
CZECHOSLOVAKIA IS NOT INVITED AND IS EFFECTIVELY SACRIFICED.

CHAMBERLAIN IS MET WITH APPLAUSE ON HIS RETURN TO ENGLAND.
RITISH
I RETURN WITH A GUARANTEE OF PEACE FOR OUR TIME!

During the remilitarization of the Rhineland in March 1936, the Führer likely overestimates the actual power of the new English sovereign. The fact is, Edward VIII sympathizes with Nazi Germany, which might explain his abdication in December, under the pretext of marrying a divorced American, Wallis Simpson, who also favors fascism and Nazism.

And if the Spanish Civil War (1936-1939) demonstrated once again European democracy's weakness against dictatorships, it also appears in hindsight as a kind of dress rehearsal for the ensuing war.

Finally, after the Anschluss in 1938, Hitler tells Mussolini he would be "eternally grateful" to him if he would accept Germany's annexation of Austria. The Duce now understands that he has become secondary to his German "ally." During the Munich Agreement in September, the Italian plays his final major role. The man who once had been a model to Hitler would henceforth be his underling.

CHAPTER

4

THE ESCALATION

1938–1939

LONDON, FALL OF 1938...

*A POLICY AIMED AT AVOIDING WAR AT ALL COSTS.

FOLLOWING THE MUNICH AGREEMENT, THE SUDETENLAND IN CZECHOSLOVAKIA IS ANNEXED TO THE REICH IN OCTOBER.

ON MARCH 14, 1939, SLOVAKIA SECEDES AT GERMANY'S INSTIGATION. MONSIGNOR JOZEF TISO, A CATHOLIC PRIEST, WOULD LEAD THE NEW REPUBLIC.
I WELCOME OUR GERMAN FRIENDS.

ON THE SAME DAY, EMIL HÁCHA, PRESIDENT OF CZECHOSLOVAKIA, IS WELCOMED IN BERLIN.
IF YOU TRY TO OPPOSE YOUR COUNTRY BEING PARTITIONED, THE GERMAN AIR FORCE WILL BOMB PRAGUE TODAY! THE PLACE WILL BE REDUCED TO ASHES!!

ON THE VERGE OF A HEART ATTACK, HÁCHA AGREES THAT WHAT IS LEFT OF HIS COUNTRY WILL BECOME A GERMAN PROTECTORATE, THE PROTECTORATE OF BOHEMIA AND MORAVIA.
FÜHRER, I-I SUBMIT TO YOUR TERMS.

THE NEXT DAY, THE GERMAN ARMY ENTERS BOHEMIA AND MORAVIA...

AND HITLER PERFORMS AN INSPECTION OF HIS TROOPS AT PRAGUE CASTLE. RECEPTION BY THE LOCAL POPULATION IS ICY.

IN ROME...
THIS TIME, THE FÜHRER CAN'T INVOKE THE RIGHT OF SELF-DETERMINATION! HE DIDN'T EVEN ASK MY OPINION.
PERHAPS, DUCE, THE TIME IS RIGHT TO START A DIALOGUE WITH FRANCE AND ENGLAND?
CERTAINLY NOT, CIANO. THE DEMOCRACIES ARE WEAK, AND HITLER IS STRONGER THAN THEY ARE.
WE'RE GOING TO GIVE HIM A TASTE OF HIS OWN MEDICINE INSTEAD.

AND ON APRIL 7, ITALY INVADES AND THEN ANNEXES ALBANIA.

NOW FASCIST ITALY CAN SPEAK WITH NATIONAL SOCIALIST GERMANY ON EQUAL FOOTING AGAIN!

ON MAY 22, 1939, IN BERLIN, ITALY'S CIANO AND THE NEW GERMAN FOREIGN MINISTER, VON RIBBENTROP, SIGN A MILITARY ALLIANCE, THE PACT OF STEEL.
FROM HERE ON OUT, GERMANY AND ITALY ARE INSEPARABLY LINKED.

IN MOSCOW, STALIN SUMMONS CHAIRMAN OF THE COUNCIL, MOLOTOV, WHO IS NOW THE USSR PEOPLE'S COMMISSAR FOR FOREIGN AFFAIRS.
WHO CAN STOP THE GERMANS NOW? FRANCE AND ENGLAND CONCEDED AT MUNICH, AND HITLER DEVOURED CZECHOSLOVAKIA WITH EASE.
COMRADE STALIN, FRANCE AND ENGLAND ARE CLEARLY NOT OPPOSING GERMANY'S EASTWARD EXPANSION. WHAT WILL THE NEXT TARGET BE? UKRAINE? POLAND?

THEN OUR TURN WILL COME. WE HAVE ONLY ONE OPTION LEFT: GET CLOSER TO THE WOLF, AT LEAST FOR A TIME!

MEANWHILE, IN LONDON...

GOOD EVENING, MR. CHAMBERLAIN.

THE OTHER CLUB MEMBERS ARE ALREADY HERE.

GOOD EVENING, NEVILLE, WE WERE JUST WAITING FOR YOU!
SO, OLD CHAP, WHAT'S THE NEWS?

WELL, YOU KNOW, NOW THAT HITLER'S GONE INTO PRAGUE, I'VE CHANGED THE DIRECTION OF OUR FOREIGN POLICY... WE GUARANTEED POLAND WE'D HELP THEM IF THEIR INDEPENDENCE WAS THREATENED... AND FRANCE HAS BACKED US.

HMM... IMAGINE, GOD FORBID, THAT GERMANY ATTACKS POLAND TOMORROW... WOULD ENGLAND DECLARE WAR ON THEM?
?!

WELL, WE'VE STARTED REARMING.
BUT, UM, WE'RE NOT QUITE READY YET.
GOD SAVE ENGLAND.
THIS WAS ABOUT BUYING TIME. AND SENDING A CLEAR SIGNAL TO HITLER IN THE MEANTIME...
THE MILITARY ASSISTANCE AGREEMENT WITH POLAND ISN'T ACTUALLY SET TO BE RATIFIED UNTIL THE END OF AUGUST.
SAY, NEVILLE, THERE ARE RUMORS THAT TALKS ARE ALSO GOING ON WITH THE SOVIET UNION.
BY GOD! TRUE, THERE ARE SOME IN THE GOVERNMENT WHO SUPPORT A RAPPROCHEMENT WITH THE USSR. BUT OF COURSE WE CANNOT MAKE A PACT WITH THE COMMUNISTS!
I ASSURE YOU, GENTLEMEN, THAT THESE NEGOTIATIONS WILL BE CONDUCTED WITH... THE UTMOST ADROITNESS.
GOOD NIGHT, GENTLEMEN!

*SEE CHAPTER 3.
**GDAŃSK, MAJOR PORT ON THE BALTIC SEA.

*SEE CHAPTER 2.

IN LONDON, CHAMBERLAIN LEARNS OF THE GERMAN-SOVIET PACT.
I'M ASTONISHED! WE MUST FINALIZE OUR MILITARY ASSISTANCE AGREEMENT WITH POLAND AS SOON AS POSSIBLE.

IN PARIS, DALADIER IS DEVASTATED...
RUSSIA HAS ABANDONED US! WE NEED TO REASSURE POLAND IMMEDIATELY.

AT BERCHTESGADEN, HITLER'S PROPERTY IN THE BAVARIAN ALPS...
MEIN FÜHRER, THE ENGLISH AMBASSADOR HENDERSON IS REQUESTING AN URGENT MEETING.
LET HIM IN!

I'VE BROUGHT A MESSAGE FROM SIR CHAMBERLAIN. WE MUST AVOID WAR AT ALL COSTS!

MR. HENDERSON, THE BRITISH ARE AT FAULT FOR ALL OF THIS. THEY WERE THE ONES WHO ENCOURAGED POLAND TO REJECT MY PROPOSALS FOR DANZIG!

ON SEPTEMBER 1, 1939, AT 4:45 IN THE MORNING, THE GERMAN AIR FORCE AND TANKS MOVE INTO POLAND, FOLLOWED BY THE INFANTRY.

THE GERMAN ADVANCE IS RUTHLESS AND UNSTOPPABLE.

THE GERMAN ARTILLERY AND AIR FORCE BOMBARD THE WESTERPLATTE PENINSULA LEADING TO THE PORT OF DANZIG...

THE GARRISON SURRENDERS ON SEPTEMBER 7, AFTER A HEROIC DEFENSE.

*MINISTER OF THE NAVY.

Did the United States play a part in starting the war? That's what Ribbentrop claims in the memoirs he wrote in his cell during the Nuremberg trials in 1945-46. He states that according to Polish reports seized in Warsaw and later in France by the Germans, President Roosevelt had decided as early as spring 1939 "not to take part at the beginning of the next conflict, but to end it." In the same vein his ambassador in Paris, Bullitt, reportedly states around the same time that, according to Roosevelt, "France and England must put an end to the politics of compromise they are practicing toward totalitarian states."

This statement would have led European democracies to believe that in the event of war with Germany, they could rely on American power for help. As early as 1917, the United States did indeed send in two million men and lent more than ten billion dollars to the Allied countries, who had been at war with the German Empire since 1914.

After Hitler's flouting of the Munich Agreement with his March 1939 occupation of Prague, England and France realize that the Führer, contrary to his pacifist proclamations, is not at all ready to halt expansion of the Reich and is even prepared to take up arms if necessary. They have very few choices left at this point. Similarly, the USSR does not have many options left, convinced–and perhaps rightly so–that the democracies would prefer to let Germany eventually clash with Russia rather than see the two countries remain allies. Stalin and Hitler had indeed caught everyone off guard. However, the alliance between communism and Nazism could only be temporary for ideological reasons.

CHAPTER

5

AWAITING THE STORM

1939–1940

ROME, AT THE PALAZZO VENEZIA, IN THE DUCE'S OFFICE...

BUT I DIDN'T EXPECT HITLER TO STRIKE POLAND SO QUICKLY, JUST AS I DIDN'T EXPECT HIM TO COLLABORATE WITH BOLSHEVIK RUSSIA!

DUCE, THERE MIGHT STILL BE TIME TO SWITCH SIDES.
YOU MUST BE JOKING, CIANO. THE FÜHRER WOULD NEVER FORGIVE ME FOR BETRAYING THE PACT OF STEEL!

THE ITALIAN DICTATOR THOUGHT ABOUT THE SITUATION LATE INTO THE NIGHT.

IF I DON'T STAND BY GERMANY, I'LL LOOK LIKE A COWARD...
AND HITLER WILL BE THE ONLY ONE TO GAIN FROM HIS VICTORIES.

BUT IF I JOIN THE CONFLICT AND GERMANY IS DEFEATED, THEN FASCIST ITALY WILL CRUMBLE...
AS WILL OUR ARMS INDUSTRY, WHICH IS LAGGING BEHIND!

AT DAWN...

IT'S DECIDED. I'M GOING TO WRITE HITLER TO TELL HIM ITALY ISN'T READY.
UNLESS GERMANY SUPPLIES US WITH EQUIPMENT... IMPOSSIBLE.

SHORTLY AFTER, IN BERLIN...
PFFT! A PATHETIC PLOY TO SHIRK HIS RESPONSIBILITIES.

IN MOSCOW, MID-SEPTEMBER...
MOLOTOV, THE GERMANS ARE REPORTEDLY AT THE GATES OF WARSAW...
IT'S OUR TURN TO ACT.

ON SEPTEMBER 17, 1939, SOVIET TROOPS MOVE INTO EASTERN POLAND WITHOUT WARNING...

THE RUSSIANS BREAK THROUGH THE POLISH RANKS, WHICH HAD ALREADY BEEN TAKEN UNAWARES AND SIGNIFICANTLY DEVASTATED BY THE GERMAN ARMY. ON SEPTEMBER 22, THE CITY OF LVIV, CAUGHT IN A VISE BETWEEN THE GERMAN AND SOVIET ARMIES, SURRENDERS. ON THE 28TH, THE SOVIET CAVALRY PARADES THROUGH THE CITY.

IN BERLIN...
THE FRENCH AND THE BRITISH HAVEN'T KEPT THEIR PROMISE TO POLAND AT ALL.
I'M VERY PLEASED ABOUT THAT, GENTLEMEN.

SO FAR, WE'VE ONLY FACED A MINOR INCURSION BY THE FRENCH NEAR SAARBRÜCKEN AND, ON SEPTEMBER 4, A BRITISH AIR RAID ON THE NAVAL BASE AT WILHELMSHAVEN.
BUT SOON, WE'LL RETALIATE BOMB FOR BOMB!

ON NOVEMBER 30, STALIN UNLEASHES THE RUSSIAN ARMY AGAINST NEIGHBORING FINLAND.

IN LONDON...

FRENCH NEWSPAPERS TALK ABOUT A "PHONEY WAR" TO DESCRIBE THE FRANCO-BRITISH WAITING ATTITUDE... YET WE HAVE NOT BEEN COMPLETELY INACTIVE. IN SEPTEMBER 1939, WE SENT AN EXPEDITIONARY FORCE OF 158,000 MEN TO FRANCE...

LE FIGARO

UNE RUÉE DE LA JEUNESSE VERS L'AVIATION

AVEC CEUX QUI N'ONT ENCORE QU'UNE AILE...

Le Gouvernement américain prépare un rapport sur la propagande allemande à l'égard des Etats-Unis

LE CONSEIL DES MINISTRES DE CE MATIN EXAMINERA LA SITUATION diplomatique et militaire

Une convention d'amitié turco-syrienne a été signée à Ankara

Attention !...

AND WE WERE PLANNING TO SEND A CONTINGENT TO AID FINLAND ALONG WITH FRANCE... TOO LATE, BECAUSE THE MOSCOW TREATY HAPPENED IN THE MEANTIME.

*LOWER CHAMBER OF THE BRITISH PARLIAMENT.

On the evening of January 30, 1939, Hitler marks his rise to power with a speech to the Reichstag–the German parliament–that includes some threatening words:

"In my life, I have often been a prophet, and most of the time, people laughed at me. During my struggle for power, it was primarily the Jewish people who met my prophecies with laughter. I prophesied that one day I would assume leadership of the German state and therefore of the people as a whole, and that then, I would solve the Jewish problem, among many others. I believe that Judaism in Germany has since choked on its own thundering laughter. Today, let me be a prophet once more: if international Jewish finance, both in Europe and abroad, succeeds once more in plunging nations into a world war, then the result will not be Bolshevization of the earth and thereby the victory of Judaism, but the annihilation of the Jewish race in Europe."

These words indicate that in the Führer's eyes, the "Jew" is leading both the capitalist world ("international finance") and the communist world ("Judeo-Bolshevism"). Annihilating the "Jewish race"–which he sees as responsible for World War I–is meant, in his mind, to save not only Germany but the entire planet. From the moment of the invasion of Poland in September 1939, the Einsatzgruppen–task forces operating in the wake of the Wehrmacht–begin massacring Jews and local officials.

In the Russian-occupied territories, other atrocities are being committed: Stalin's idea is to rule through terror by "cleansing" Polish society. Fifteen thousand prisoners of war are massacred by the NKVD, the political police under the ministry of internal affairs. In the Katyn Forest, in April 1940, 4,100 Polish army officers are executed and buried in a mass grave, a crime that would long be attributed to the Nazis.

CHAPTER

6

THUNDER IN THE WEST

1940

BRUSSELS, AT DAWN, MAY 10, 1940...
VRROOOMMMM
WHAT?!
THE GERMANS ARE BACK.
THE BOCHES ARE HERE!
THOUSANDS OF BELGIANS FLEE TO FRANCE, HOPING TO FIND SAFE HAVEN THERE.
IN JUST EIGHTEEN DAYS, THE BELGIAN ARMY, UNDER THE COMMAND OF KING LEOPOLD III, IS FORCED TO SURRENDER. THE GERMAN BLITZKRIEG IS A SUCCESS. THE NETHERLANDS AND LUXEMBOURG ARE ALSO INVADED.

*SECRETARY OF FOREIGN AFFAIRS IN CHAMBERLAIN'S GOVERNMENT.

*GEORGE VI, KING SINCE DECEMBER 11, 1936.

ON MAY 13, 1940, SEVEN GERMAN ARMORED DIVISIONS SWEEP THROUGH THE ARDENNES, BETWEEN DINANT AND SEDAN. NO FRENCH TANKS ARE THERE TO OPPOSE THEM ON THIS PART OF THE FRONT.

*METHAMPHETAMINE.

THAT AFTERNOON, IN LONDON, AT PARLIAMENT...

IT'S AS IF DESTINY AND I ARE NOW ONE. MY ENTIRE LIFE HAS BEEN NOTHING MORE THAN PREPARATION FOR THIS MOMENT!

CHURCHILL SPEAKS BEFORE THE HOUSE OF COMMONS.
WE ARE IN THE PRELIMINARY STAGE OF ONE OF THE GREATEST BATTLES IN HISTORY... I HAVE NOTHING TO OFFER BUT BLOOD, TOIL, TEARS, AND SWEAT.

YOU ASK, WHAT IS OUR POLICY?
IT IS TO WAGE WAR, BY SEA, LAND, AND AIR...
YOU ASK, WHAT IS OUR AIM?
IT IS VICTORY, VICTORY AT ALL COSTS.

AFTER BREAKING THROUGH THE FRONT AT SEDAN AND CROSSING THE MEUSE ON MAY 14, THE GERMANS RACE TOWARD THE BAIE DE SOMME. IT SEEMS AS IF NOTHING CAN SLOW THEIR ADVANCE.

THE NEXT DAY, CHURCHILL HEADS TO PARIS.

THE SITUATION IS MORE SERIOUS THAN I THOUGHT...
THE GERMANS ARE CLOSE TO REACHING THE SOMME!

ALL RIGHT, I'LL SEND YOU TEN ADDITIONAL FIGHTER SQUADRONS...
BUT I NEED TO KEEP TWENTY-FIVE OF THEM IN ORDER TO PROTECT ENGLAND!

IT'S NO USE... ON MAY 20, THE 2ND PANZER DIVISION, LED BY GUDERIAN, REACHES ABBEVILLE, WHICH HAS BEEN BOMBARDED BY THE LUFTWAFFE.
IN THE EVENING, ONE OF THE ARMORED BATTALIONS REACHES THE ENGLISH CHANNEL COAST. HITLER IS OVERJOYED TO HEAR THE NEWS!

*BRITISH EXPEDITIONARY FORCE.

FROM MAY 26 TO JUNE 4, IN DUNKIRK, UNDER GERMAN AIR ASSAULT, MILITARY AND CIVILIAN BOATS COMING FROM ENGLAND MANAGE TO EVACUATE OVER 330,000 ALLIED SOLDIERS...

OPERATION DYNAMO PUTS AN END TO THE FRANCO-BRITISH ALLIANCE ON THE GROUND.

The *Haltbefehl*—the order to halt given to the panzer divisions on May 24, 1940, which allowed the evacuation of 198,229 British, 139,997 French, and 16,816 Belgians to England–remains as one of the most controversial elements of World War II. According to historian Antony Beevor, Hitler does not personally give this order; he merely approves it. The fact is that re-embarkation does take place, in hellish conditions, as depicted in the films *Weekend at Dunkirk* by Henri Verneuil (1964) and *Dunkirk* by Christopher Nolan (2017).

There are two main opposing theses. According to the first, it's the political will of Germany to separate the French and the British, in order to reach a separate peace with Britain (this is the thesis defended by historian François Delpla, for example). Another hypothesis is that it's about allowing the German armored divisions some time to breathe after their blitz through France. They came into marshy land and risked running out of logistical supplies. Göring's bravado might have done the rest.

Meanwhile, King Leopold III of Belgium surrenders on May 28; to the French and the English, he is a convenient scapegoat, with Churchill blaming Belgium's "fatal neutrality" in his June 4 speech to the House of Commons. It is worth mentioning that this speech ends with England's commitment to continue fighting until "the New World, with all its power and might steps forth to the rescue and the liberation of the Old." America's involvement is nevertheless not a guarantee...

CHAPTER

7

THIS IS LONDON!

1940–1941

ON JUNE 6, 1940, AT 1:30 P.M., THE FÜHRER AND HIS ENTOURAGE ARRIVE NEAR THE HAMLET OF BRÛLY-DE-PESCHE, CLOSE TO COUVIN IN BELGIUM, WHERE HIS MAIN HEADQUARTERS HAS BEEN SET UP.
ALL THE RESIDENTS FROM THE SURROUNDING VILLAGES MUST LEAVE THEIR HOMES.

*"WOLFSSCHANZE" IN GERMAN.

NOW THAT WE ARE ON THE VERGE OF FORCING THE FRENCH TO SURRENDER, HE WANTS TO JOIN IN OUR VICTORY?

THAT'S WHY I TOLD OUR "ALLY" TO WAIT A BIT. ITALY WILL ONLY OFFICIALLY ENTER THE WAR ON JUNE 10 AT MIDNIGHT.
THAT GIVES US TIME TO FINISH THIS!

UP UNTIL JUNE 12, THE FRENCH, OUTNUMBERED BY THE GERMANS, PUT UP A HEROIC RESISTANCE ON THE SOMME AND THE AISNE.

BUT ON THE 12TH, FRENCH TROOPS ARE FORCED TO RETREAT TO THE SEINE AND THE MARNE... ON THE 14TH, THE GERMANS ARE IN PARIS!

THE FRENCH GOVERNMENT HAS WITHDRAWN TO BORDEAUX...

PAUL REYNAUD HAS BEEN CONSULTING WITH PHILIPPE PÉTAIN, WHO WAS APPOINTED TO THE GOVERNMENT AS VICE-PRESIDENT OF THE COUNCIL ON MAY 18...

*BATTLE WON BY THE FRENCH IN 1916.

ON JUNE 16, AT 9:30 P.M., RETURNING FROM A MISSION IN LONDON, BRIGADIER GENERAL CHARLES DE GAULLE, UNDER SECRETARY OF STATE FOR WAR SINCE JUNE 6, LANDS IN BORDEAUX.

HE IMMEDIATELY GOES TO SEE PAUL REYNAUD.
THE GERMAN BREAKTHROUGH AT SEDAN, THE DISASTER AT DUNKIRK, PARIS DELIVERED TO THE INVADER... I AM COMPLETELY DISILLUSIONED. I'VE RESIGNED AND HAVE TASKED PÉTAIN WITH FORMING A NEW GOVERNMENT.
AH!

THE MARSHAL, WHO IS AN OLD MAN, WILL CERTAINLY CONSIDER THE ENEMY'S TERMS...
AS FOR ME, I'M HEADING BACK TO LONDON TO CONTINUE THE FIGHT!

HERE ARE 100,000 FRANCS TAKEN FROM OUR SECRET FUNDS.

ON THE 17TH, AT 9 A.M., DE GAULLE FLIES TO ENGLAND.

THAT VERY AFTERNOON, HE MEETS WITH CHURCHILL...
MY INTENTION IS TO CONTINUE THE WAR...

BUT HOW?!
IN THE NAME OF FRANCE, FOR THE NATIONAL SALVATION OF MY COUNTRY!

HMM...ALL RIGHT, I'LL ARRANGE FOR THE BBC TO BE AT YOUR DISPOSAL AS SOON AS PÉTAIN REQUESTS AN ARMISTICE WITH THE GERMANS.

THAT EVENING...
IT'S DONE, GENERAL! THE MARSHAL HAS CALLED FOR A CEASEFIRE IN FRANCE.

THE NEXT DAY, AT 6 P.M., DE GAULLE SPEAKS INTO THE BBC MICROPHONE FOR THE "APPEAL OF JUNE 18."
IS DEFEAT FINAL? NO! THIS WAR IS NOT FINISHED BY THE BATTLE OF FRANCE; THIS WAR IS A WORLD WIDE WAR... I INVITE THE OFFICERS AND THE FRENCH SOLDIERS WHO ARE LOCATED IN BRITISH TERRITORY TO PUT THEMSELVES IN CONTACT WITH ME...

ON JUNE 22, 1940, THE FRENCH DELEGATION SIGNS THE ARMISTICE IN COMPIÈGNE. A FEW MONTHS LATER, PÉTAIN WOULD CALL ON THE POPULATION TO COLLABORATE WITH THE THIRD REICH.

AT DAWN ON THE 23RD, HITLER IS IN PARIS, ACCOMPANIED BY ARCHITECTS SPEER AND GIESLER, AND SCULPTOR ARNO BREKER...
I WANT TO SEE THE OPERA GARNIER FIRST, MY FAVORITE BUILDING!

THE FÜHRER ORDERS THEM TO A HALT BEFORE THE EIFFEL TOWER.

AT LES INVALIDES, HE REFLECTS FOR A LONG TIME BEFORE NAPOLEON'S TOMB.
AT 9 A.M., HITLER BOARDS A PLANE AT LE BOURGET. BY 10 A.M., HE'S BACK AT HIS HQ IN BRÛLY-DE-PESCHE.

FRENCH BATTLESHIPS AND DESTROYERS ARE ANCHORED AT MERS EL-KÉBIR,** IN THE BAY OF ORAN. ON JULY 3, 1940, AT DAWN, THE BRITISH OFFER ADMIRAL GENSOUL THE CHANCE TO JOIN A BRITISH PORT OR A FRENCH CARIBBEAN PORT. THE FRENCHMAN REFUSES, AND AT 5:55 P.M., THE ROYAL NAVY OPENS FIRE.

FRENCH SHIPS ARE BOMBARDED AND SUNK; 1,295 SAILORS ARE KILLED.

*HE WOULD SETTLE IN VICHY ON JULY 10.
**THE "GREAT PORT" IN ARABIC.

ON JULY 10, THE BATTLE OF BRITAIN BEGINS. THE LUFTWAFFE, UNDER REICHSMARSCHALL GÖRING'S COMMAND, AIMS TO ANNIHILATE THE ENGLISH AIR FORCE AND TERRORIZE THE POPULATION BY BOMBING THE CITIES.

BUT THE ROYAL AIR FORCE'S SPITFIRE SQUADRONS PERSIST IN HOLDING OUT. WHILE THE BRITS GRIT THEIR TEETH, HITLER GROWS FRUSTRATED AND SOON SHIFTS FOCUS. THE LAST GERMAN RAIDS TAKE PLACE ON MAY 10, 1941.

Churchill's war diaries depict his government as united. However, there were cracks beneath this smooth surface: some members of the government, like Halifax, were not entirely opposed to negotiating a separate peace treaty with Germany. A recent film, *The Darkest Hour* by Joe Wright (2017), portrays the challenges faced by the prime minister in achieving national unity in May and June of 1940.

As for Hitler, does he merely aim to occupy the "Fortress Europe" and leave the English–considered by Nazi racial theory as cousins to the Germans–to rule a colonial empire that was then one of the most powerful in the world? It's hard to say: the halting of the panzers before Dunkirk, and subsequent to that, the apparent abandonment in May 1941 of the Führer's plans to conquer Great Britain, suggest this might be the case. Nevertheless, Churchill is convinced otherwise, and as early as June 4, 1940, he speaks of Hitler's "invasion plan" for the British Isles; an idea he claims "is not new," since Napoleon had once considered it, too. With no significant show of resilience by the British, one might indeed wonder how the conflict would turn out.

The notion of continuing the war alone (with the fragile alliance of de Gaulle, advocate of a "Free France," from London) is only justifiable for England by the possibility of eventual intervention by the Americans. De Gaulle, in his Appeal of June 18, even refers to the "vast industry of the United States..."

Mers el-Kébir of course leads to a wave of Anglophobia in France. Admiral Darlan and Deputy Prime Minister Laval want France to declare war on the English. Pétain allegedly replies, "One defeat is enough!"

From London, de Gaulle aims to unify the resistance in France by sending former prefect Jean Moulin there in early 1942 (in '43, he would be captured and tortured by the gestapo, the state secret police). Across Nazi-occupied Europe, resistance movements emerge from widely varied, and sometimes opposing, political backgrounds.

CHAPTER

THE DUCE GOES TO WAR

1940–1941

ITALY DECLARES WAR AGAINST FRANCE AND ENGLAND ON JUNE 10. LED BY PRINCE UMBERTO OF SAVOY, THE ITALIANS ATTACK THE FRENCH IN THE ALPS, WITH THE LATTER INFLICTING HEAVY LOSSES.

HOWEVER, ON JUNE 25, IN ROME, THE FRANCO-ITALIAN ARMISTICE IS SIGNED: IT COMES AFTER THE ARMISTICE FRANCE SIGNED WITH GERMANY ON THE 22ND. FROM THIS POINT ON, ITALY BENEFITS FROM A SMALL OCCUPATION ZONE IN THE MARITIME ALPS, INCLUDING MENTON.

DURING THE BATTLE OF BRITAIN, ITALIAN FIGHTER PILOTS GO INTO COMBAT ALONGSIDE THE GERMANS.

*THE FASCIST PARTY, ESTABLISHED THROUGHOUT ITALY.

I KNOW THAT, CIANO. THE ITALIANS MIGHT BE PESSIMISTIC, BUT GERMANY IS WINNING THIS WAR! AND WE CAN'T BE LEFT BEHIND.
THE GLORY OF ITALY REQUIRES US TO STAND BESIDE OUR POWERFUL ALLY.

CIANO, I'M ENTRUSTING YOU TO GO AND CONVINCE THE FÜHRER; WE MUST PARTICIPATE IN THE INVASION OF ENGLAND!

BERLIN, JULY 19, THE NEW REICH CHANCELLERY...

COUNT CIANO, THE FÜHRER WILL SEE YOU NOW!

*OPERATION SEA LION.

ON SEPTEMBER 9, 1940, THE ITALIAN AIR FORCE ATTACKS THE ROYAL AIR FORCE IN EGYPT AND LIBYA.

THE DUCE CONTACTS GENERAL GRAZIANI, WHOM BADOGLIO HAS TASKED WITH INVADING EGYPT—WHERE 40,000 BRITISH SOLDIERS ARE STATIONED—AND WITH TAKING THE SUEZ CANAL...
GRAZIANI, IT'S HIGH TIME TO LAUNCH THE OFFENSIVE! IF YOU KEEP STALLING, I'LL HAVE YOU REMOVED!

ON SEPTEMBER 13, GRAZIANI, FROM NEIGHBORING LIBYA, MANAGES A BREAKTHROUGH INTO EGYPTIAN TERRITORY.

MUSSOLINI, TRIUMPHANT, REFUSES THE HELP OF THE TANK DIVISIONS HITLER OFFERS. IN DECEMBER, THE BRITISH, LED BY GENERAL WAVELL, LAUNCH A SUCCESSFUL COUNTERATTACK.
THE ITALIAN OFFENSIVE IS A CRUSHING FAILURE.

*SEE CHAPTER 3.
** "THE LEADER," TITLE GIVEN TO FRANCO.

THE FOLLOWING EVENING, THE FÜHRER'S SPECIAL TRAIN STOPS IN FRANCE, AT MONTOIRE STATION...

PÉTAIN AND HIS MINISTER LAVAL ARE WELCOMED ABOARD HITLER'S PARLOR CAR, JOINED BY RIBBENTROP...
GOOD EVENING, MARSHAL.
I REGRET THAT FRANCE DECLARED WAR ON GERMANY IN '39. WE MUST ATONE FOR THIS MADNESS...

I SPOKE WITH THE FÜHRER ABOUT A POSSIBLE COLLABORATION BETWEEN OUR TWO COUNTRIES... AND, LET ME REMIND YOU, WE HAVE SENTENCED THAT RENEGADE, DE GAULLE, TO DEATH!
I ACCEPT THE PRINCIPLE OF COLLABORATION. WE JUST NEED TO WORK OUT THE DETAILS.

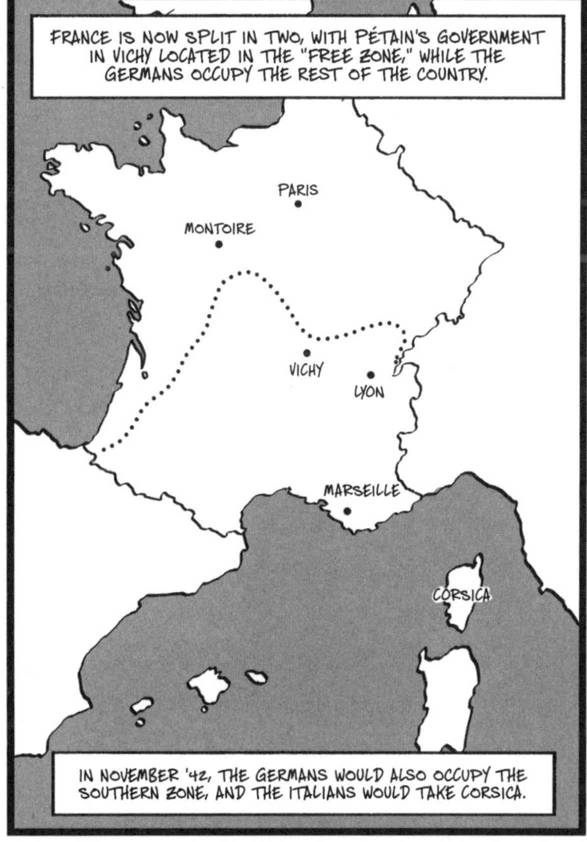
FRANCE IS NOW SPLIT IN TWO, WITH PÉTAIN'S GOVERNMENT IN VICHY LOCATED IN THE "FREE ZONE," WHILE THE GERMANS OCCUPY THE REST OF THE COUNTRY.
PARIS
MONTOIRE
VICHY
LYON
MARSEILLE
CORSICA
IN NOVEMBER '42, THE GERMANS WOULD ALSO OCCUPY THE SOUTHERN ZONE, AND THE ITALIANS WOULD TAKE CORSICA.

HAVING FAILED IN NORTH AFRICA, MUSSOLINI WANTS TO START HIS WAR IN THE BALKANS...
LET'S ATTACK YUGOSLAVIA!
HITLER WILL OPPOSE IT: PRINCE REGENT PAUL OF YUGOSLAVIA HAS GOTTEN CLOSER WITH GERMANY. GREECE, ON THE OTHER HAND, IS NEUTRAL.

AH...OCCUPYING IT WOULD INDEED WEAKEN THE BRITISH FLEET IN THE AEGEAN SEA...AND THEIR BASES IN EGYPT!

STARTING FROM NEIGHBORING ALBANIA AND WITH TOO FEW MEN LED BY GENERAL PRASCA, THE OFFENSIVE BEGINS ON OCTOBER 28, 1940. THE GREEK TROOPS PUT UP A FIERCE RESISTANCE AND ARE SOON SUPPORTED BY THE BRITISH.

IN JANUARY 1941, HITLER DECIDES TO INTERVENE. BY THE END OF APRIL, THE GERMANS TAKE ATHENS.

IN YUGOSLAVIA, THE RESISTANCE FIGHTERS GO UP AGAINST THE OCCUPIERS, SPLIT BETWEEN MIHAILOVIĆ'S SERBIAN ROYALISTS AND TITO'S COMMUNISTS.*

ON MAY 20, 1941, GERMAN PARATROOPERS UNDER THE LEADERSHIP OF GENERAL STUDENT DROP INTO THE ISLAND OF CRETE, THE LAST BASTION DEFENDED BY THE GREEKS WITH SUPPORT FROM THE BRITISH AND NEW ZEALAND.

FOUR THOUSAND PARATROOPERS ARE KILLED, BUT THE REICH'S MOUNTAIN TROOPS EVENTUALLY WIN THE BATTLE. FROM MAY 27 TO JUNE 1, THE ALLIES EVACUATE THE ISLAND—A VERY COSTLY VICTORY FOR THE FÜHRER.

*POLITICAL, ETHNIC, AND RELIGIOUS DIVISIONS WOULD RESURFACE IN THE COUNTRY AFTER TITO'S DEATH IN 1980.

If the Italian attempt to invade Egypt in September 1940 marks the first episode of the desert war, the Battle of Crete, from May 20 to June 1, 1941, is the last episode of the Balkan campaign.

According to a source whose authenticity is still debated, Hitler allegedly states in February '45: "Without the difficulties created by the Italians with their foolish Greek campaign, I would have attacked the Russians a few weeks earlier." (*Hitler's Political Testament, notes collected by Martin Bormann*, Favard, 1959, p. 95.)

And also: "That [the Italian campaign against Greece] led us, contrary to all our plans, to intervene in the Balkans, resulting in a catastrophic delay in launching the war against Russia." (Ibid., p. 105)

Authentic or not, these statements have persisted over time. Is the Duce truly responsible for Germany's defeat? We shall now attempt to understand why and how the Führer, who claimed he would not make the mistake of waging a two-front war, launches his Russian campaign, just like Napolean before him.

CHAPTER

TOWARD BARBAROSSA

1940–1941

MOSCOW, EARLY JUNE 1940. THE KREMLIN, A FORTRESS AT THE HEART OF THE CITY, HAS BEEN THE SEAT OF POWER FROM THE TIME OF THE CZARS TO JOSEPH STALIN, AND STILL IS TODAY.

COMRADE STALIN, THIS IS IMPORTANT...

REPORTS FROM OUR SPIES ALL INDICATE THAT, AFTER DEFEATING FRANCE, GERMANY INTENDS TO TURN AGAINST US...

HMM...

CAN WE REALLY TRUST OUR AGENTS ABROAD?!

COME NOW, COMRADE MOLOTOV. HITLER ISN'T CRAZY ENOUGH TO TRY TO DOMINATE THE WORLD! HE WON'T FIGHT A WAR ON TWO FRONTS... BUT LET'S SLOW DOWN OUR DEALINGS WITH THE REICH...

*CHIEF OF THE OKW, THE HIGH COMMAND OF THE WEHRMACHT.

SPEER, THE TIME HAS COME TO SERIOUSLY CONFRONT BOLSHEVISM!

ATTACK SOVIET RUSSIA... AND WHAT ABOUT ENGLAND, MEIN FÜHRER?

EXACTLY. THE BRITISH ARE WAITING FOR U.S. ASSISTANCE, WHICH WON'T BE READY FOR ANOTHER TWO OR THREE YEARS.
IF, IN THE MEANTIME, LONDON WERE TO COZY UP TO MOSCOW, WE'D BE FINISHED, SPEER!

THAT'S WHY WE MUST ACT IN THE EAST WITHOUT DELAY! BELIEVE ME, GIVEN STALIN'S PURGING OF THE RED ARMY AND THE WEAKNESS OF THE JUDEO-BOLSHEVIK STATE, THIS CAMPAIGN WILL BE CHILD'S PLAY.

MOSCOW, EARLY NOVEMBER...

OUR RELATIONS WITH BERLIN ARE AT AN ALL-TIME LOW, COMRADE STALIN. RIBBENTROP IS PROPOSING A MEETING WITH HITLER IN BERLIN.
?!

HA HA! IT SEEMS OUR RECENT CONTACTS WITH THE ENGLISH AMBASSADOR, CRIPPS, ARE BEARING FRUIT: THE FÜHRER IS GETTING WORRIED... VERY GOOD, COMRADE MOLOTOV, GO AHEAD AND FEEL THINGS OUT IN BERLIN.

BE SURE TO TELL THEM WE WANT TO GET INVOLVED IN FINLAND AS WELL AS BULGARIA... AND TRY TO SEE IF THEY ARE CONSIDERING AN ALLIANCE WITH LONDON AGAINST US!

ON NOVEMBER 12, 1940, IN LATE MORNING, MOLOTOV AND THE SOVIET DELEGATION ARRIVE IN BERLIN.
WELCOME TO THE REICH, MR. MOLOTOV!
GOOD TO SEE YOU AGAIN, HERR RIBBENTROP.

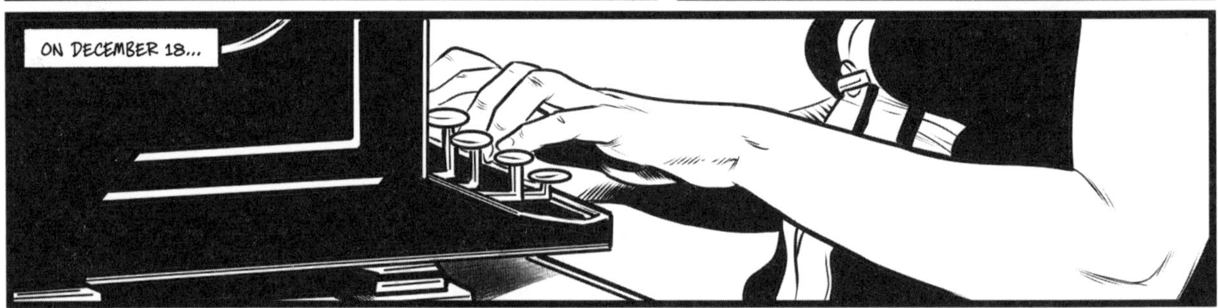

*RUDOLF HESS, DEPUTY TO THE FÜHRER.
**NAMED AFTER GERMANIC EMPEROR BARBAROSSA, WHO DIED DURING THE CRUSADES IN 1190.

IN LATE JANUARY 1941, THERE IS A DINNER HOSTED BY VON BRAUCHITSCH, THE COMMANDER IN CHIEF OF THE ARMY. GENERAL HALDER AND HIS DEPUTY ARE IN ATTENDANCE, AS WELL AS VON LEEB, VON BOCK, AND VON RUNDSTEDT.
WELCOME, MY FRIENDS!
AFTER THE MEAL...
BETWEEN US, GENTLEMEN, IS THE PLAN FOR THE CAMPAIGN WE'RE GOING TO LEAD IN THE EAST A STRATEGIC ONE OR AN IDEOLOGICAL STRIKE?
HALDER, WHAT'S YOUR TAKE ON IT?
IN MY OPINION, CONTRARY TO WHAT HITLER CLAIMS, TAKING MOSCOW WON'T CAUSE LONDON TO YIELD; THEY'RE WAITING FOR ASSISTANCE FROM THE UNITED STATES. WHAT DO YOU THINK, VON RUNDSTEDT?
ACH... WE'VE ALL SWORN ALLEGIANCE TO THE FÜHRER, MEINE HERREN. *BEFEHL IST BEFEHL!* AN ORDER IS AN ORDER.

*SEE THE END OF CHAPTER 8.

THIRTY MINUTES AFTER THE INVASION BEGINS...
THIS IS GENERAL ZHUKOV SPEAKING. I'M REQUESTING COMMUNICATION WITH COMRADE STALIN...

RING
RING

COMRADE STALIN! THE GERMANS ARE ATTACKING US!
...

COMRADE STALIN, ARE YOU HEARING ME?

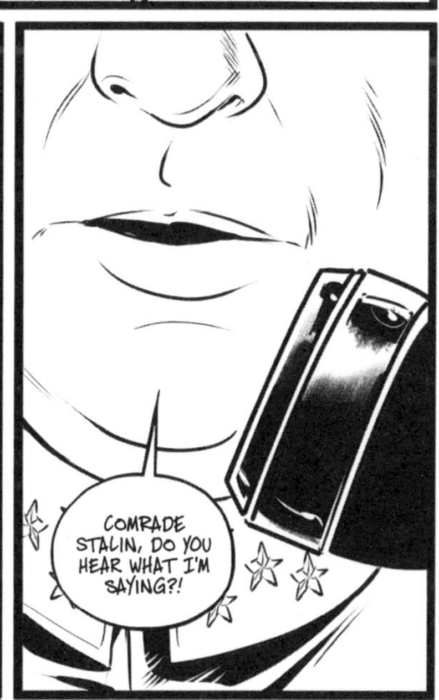
COMRADE STALIN, DO YOU HEAR WHAT I'M SAYING?!

The dismemberment of Czechoslovakia and the occupation of Poland can be seen as preliminary steps in the "great march eastward" that Hitler envisioned as early as his writing of *Mein Kampf* in 1924–1925. The Führer continuously adapts to circumstances, seizing opportunities that arise. However, his ultimate goals remain unchanged: exact revenge for the defeat of 1918 by crushing France, destroy Soviet Russia—and, after that, just Russia in its entirety (waging an "extermination war" in the east to free up vast territories for future German soldier-colonists)—and finally eliminate the "Jewry." Given the Nazi delusions of a "Judeo-Bolshevik plot," these last two objectives align perfectly...

The German-Soviet pact, in this sense, was purely tactical. Faced with the blockade imposed from the start of the war by the mighty British navy, finding new access to vital raw materials becomes increasingly necessary. In exchange, the USSR gains access to machinery and technological processes it had previously lacked. At the start of Barbarossa, the scales were seriously tipped in Germany's favor; by this point, Hitler seeks to seize direct control.

CHAPTER

VICTORY IN THE EAST?

1941

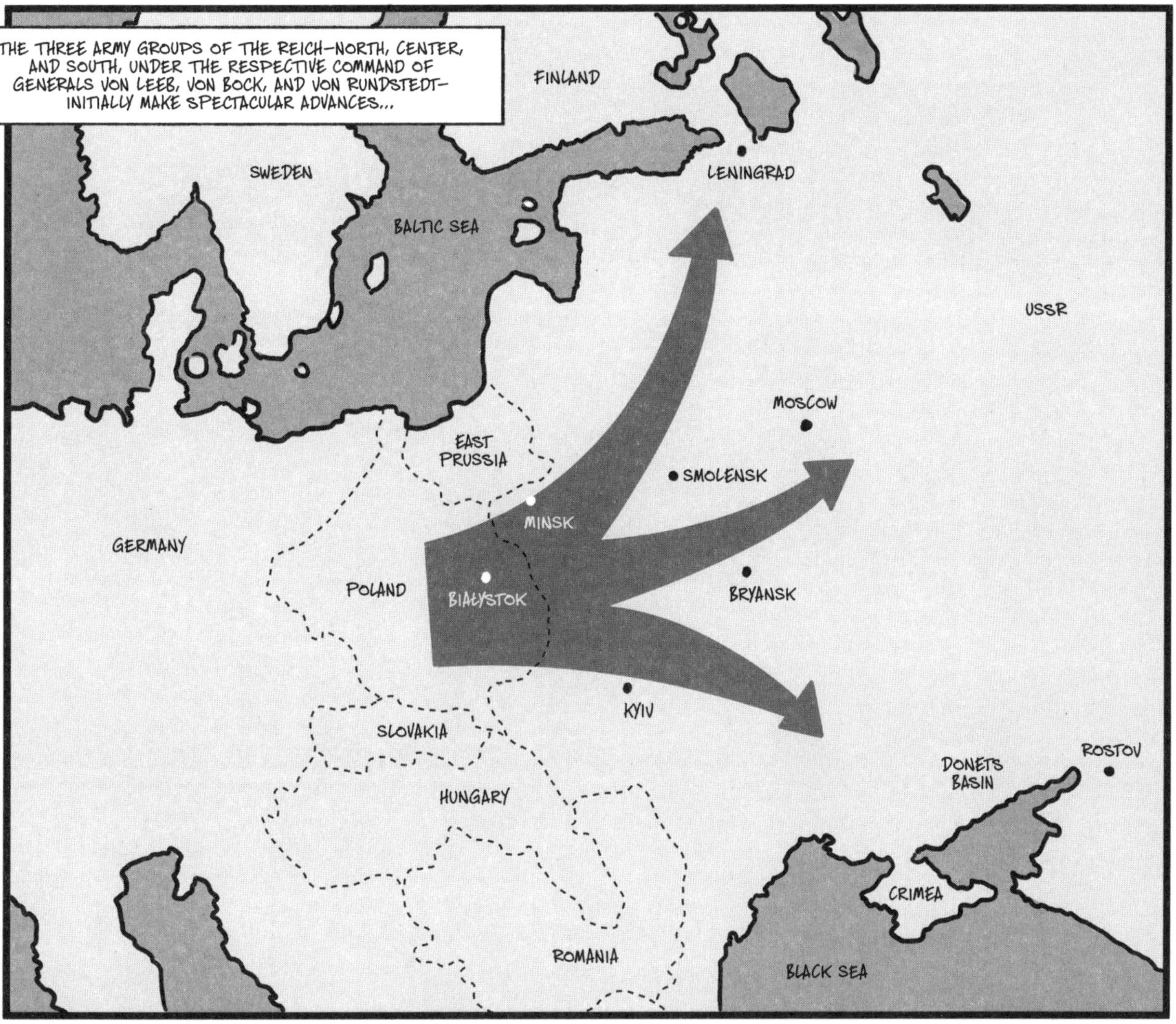

THE THREE ARMY GROUPS OF THE REICH—NORTH, CENTER, AND SOUTH, UNDER THE RESPECTIVE COMMAND OF GENERALS VON LEEB, VON BOCK, AND VON RUNDSTEDT—INITIALLY MAKE SPECTACULAR ADVANCES...

FINLAND
SWEDEN
LENINGRAD
BALTIC SEA
USSR
MOSCOW
EAST PRUSSIA
SMOLENSK
MINSK
GERMANY
POLAND
BIAŁYSTOK
BRYANSK
KYIV
SLOVAKIA
ROSTOV
DONETS BASIN
HUNGARY
CRIMEA
ROMANIA
BLACK SEA

VON RUNDSTEDT'S MISSION IS TO SEIZE UKRAINE, THE BREADBASKET OF EUROPE...
WE CANNOT END UP STARVED LIKE IN THE LAST WAR!

BUT THE RUSSIAN GENERAL KIRPONOS, WITH THE BULK OF THE SOVIET TROOPS AND THEIR BEST TANKS, RESIST THE ADVANCE OF THE SOUTH ARMY.

IN THE WOLF'S LAIR, HITLER'S HQ IN RASTENBURG, EAST PRUSSIA...
THE SOVIET SUPPLY OF MEN AND WEAPONS SEEMS ENDLESS... VICTORY APPEARS TO BE SLIPPING AWAY.

IT'S OUT OF THE QUESTION! I AM ORDERING THE PANZER DIVISIONS OF THE CENTER ARMY COMMANDED BY GUDERIAN TO CONCENTRATE HEAVILY IN THE KYIV REGION.
ONCE THIS POCKET OF RESISTANCE IS ELIMINATED, WE'LL RESUME THE MARCH TOWARD MOSCOW...
A DECISION THAT WOULD STALL THE FRONT FOR OVER A MONTH, ALLOWING THE RUSSIANS TO PREPARE FOR THE BATTLE OF MOSCOW.

ON SEPTEMBER 29 AND 30, 1941, OVER 30,000 JEWS FROM KYIV WOULD BE GATHERED TOGETHER AND TRANSPORTED TO THE BABI YAR RAVINE.

THERE, THEY WOULD BE EXECUTED BY GERMAN MARKSMEN FROM A SPECIAL COMMANDO,* AIDED BY UKRAINIAN AUXILIARIES. SOME MEMBERS OF THE WEHRMACHT WOULD PARTICIPATE IN CONCEALING THE BODIES.

*SONDERKOMMANDO 4A COMMANDED BY BLOBEL.

WHILE THE MAIN GERMAN FORCES REGROUP TOWARD THE CENTER FOR OPERATION TYPHOON TARGETING MOSCOW, WHAT REMAINS OF ARMY GROUP SOUTH WOULD, ON NOVEMBER 20, TAKE ROSTOV-ON-DON.

THIS MAJOR INDUSTRIAL CITY AND STRATEGIC POINT IN SOUTHERN RUSSIA IS A CRUCIAL GATEWAY ON THE ROUTE TO THE CAUCASUS OIL FIELDS.

MEANWHILE, ARMY GROUP CENTER, LED BY VON BOCK, HAS MADE PROGRESS AT LIGHTNING SPEED...
IF THIS CONTINUES, WE'LL SOON BE WITHIN SIGHT OF MOSCOW, AND IF THE CITY FALLS, THE RUSSIAN STATE WILL COLLAPSE.

THREE HUNDRED THOUSAND SOVIET SOLDIERS ARE CAPTURED N BIAŁYSTOK, AS WELL AS IN THE MINSK "POCKET."

WHAT WAS GOING ON AT THE KREMLIN ALL THIS TIME?
I'M GOING TO HAVE GENERAL PAVLOV SHOT. THAT INCOMPETENT MAN COULDN'T STOP THE GERMAN ADVANCE!

DMITRI PAVLOV IS EXECUTED BY THE NKVD ON JULY 22, 1941.

THE GERMANS TAKE SMOLENSK ON JULY 16, ON THE WAY TO MOSCOW, DESPITE RESISTANCE FROM GENERAL TIMOSHENKO.

AROUND MID-OCTOBER 1941, THE CITIES OF VYAZMA AND BRYANSK, WHERE THE LAST OF THE SOVIET FORCES GATHERED BEFORE REACHING MOSCOW, ALSO FALL INTO GERMAN HANDS AFTER BEING TWICE SURROUNDED...

MOSCOW IS IN COMPLETE PANIC! RESIDENTS START FLEEING AS THE GERMANS MAKE THEIR WAY CLOSER, WHILE THE NKVD, UNDER STALIN'S COMMAND, EXECUTE DESERTERS AND PLUNDERERS, AND THE PANZERS CONTINUE THEIR SEEMINGLY UNSTOPPABLE ADVANCE...
MUSCOVITES ARE BEING RECRUITED EN MASSE TO DIG TRENCHES...
AT THE KREMLIN...
IF I LEAVE MOSCOW NOW, WE'RE DONE FOR... BUT IF I STAY, I RISK BEING CAPTURED AND KILLED BY THE NAZIS!

*SEE CHAPTER 2.
**MINUS SIX DEGREES FAHRENHEIT.

*FOURTEEN MILES.
**MINUS THIRTY-ONE DEGREES FAHRENHEIT.

A German propaganda pamphlet loudly proclaims: "Victory in the east." But they jumped the Soviet gun.

Setting out from occupied Poland, the massive offensive launched by Hitler—which his Italian, Finnish, Romanian, Croatian, Slovak, and Hungarian allies joined, as well as voluntary recruits in the Waffen-SS from Belgium, France, and others—Operation Barbarossa, which German propaganda minister Goebbels dubs a "European crusade against Bolshevism," ultimately fails due to an unrelenting Russian resistance. Of the Führer's three objectives—Moscow, Ukraine, and Leningrad—capturing only the second is achieved by the fall of '41.

The campaign reaches a new level of horror: the massive execution of Jews in the Babi Yar ravine marks the beginning of the "Holocaust by Bullets." Was this part of a preestablished plan? The question remains unclear, and we will come back to it.

On the Soviet side, facing the threat posed to the Communist state by an initially lightning-quick advance by the German armies, dictator Stalin decides to mobilize the population by addressing the Russians as his "brothers" and "sisters," appealing to national sentiment (in a speech on July 3, 1941). Henceforth, it would be called the "Great Patriotic War" in Russia.

If Barbarossa, the German offensive in the east, marks a turning point in the conflict, yet another pivotal moment will soon emerge...

CHAPTER

AMERICA AT WAR

1941

ON DECEMBER 8, 1941, AT 1 P.M., TWO DAYS AFTER ZHUKOV'S COUNTEROFFENSIVE BEGINS IN RUSSIA, AMERICAN PRESIDENT ROOSEVELT ADDRESSES THE UNITED STATES CONGRESS...
YESTERDAY, DECEMBER 7, 1941— A DATE WHICH WILL LIVE IN INFAMY—THE UNITED STATES OF AMERICA WAS SUDDENLY AND DELIBERATELY ATTACKED BY NAVAL AND AIR FORCES OF THE EMPIRE OF JAPAN.

HOSTILITIES EXIST. THERE IS NO BLINKING AT THE FACT THAT OUR PEOPLE, OUR TERRITORY, AND OUR INTERESTS ARE IN GRAVE DANGER.

I ASK THAT THE CONGRESS DECLARE THAT SINCE THE UNPROVOKED ATTACK, A STATE OF WAR HAS EXISTED BETWEEN THE UNITED STATES AND THE JAPANESE EMPIRE.
HOORAY
HOORAY
HOORAY
HOORAY
CONGRESS VOTES IMMEDIATELY FOR A DECLARATION OF WAR, AND ON DECEMBER 11, GERMANY AND ITALY, JAPAN'S ALLIES, DECLARE WAR ON AMERICA. HOW DID IT COME TO THIS?

JUST A LITTLE LESS THAN A YEAR AND A HALF EARLIER, WHEN FRANCE SIGNS THE ARMISTICE ON JUNE 22, 1940, AFTER ITS DEFEAT BY GERMANY, ROOSEVELT IN WASHINGTON IS DISMAYED.
THIS IS THE WORST POSSIBLE SCENARIO: GERMANY TO THE WEST, THE USSR TO THE EAST, NOW DOMINATING EUROPE...

BOTH CHURCHILL AND DE GAULLE HAVE PLACED ALL THEIR HOPES IN THE UNITED STATES, AND THE AMERICAN PRESIDENT KNOWS IT...
FOR NOW, I CAN DO NOTHING: AMERICAN PUBLIC OPINION IS AGAINST GOING TO WAR...

BUT I CAN SUPPORT ON THE EQUIPMENT FRONT!

MR. CHURCHILL, OUR INDUSTRY CAN HELP YOU RESIST THE GERMANS... PROVIDED GREAT BRITAIN HAS THE MEANS, OF COURSE.
WE CAN OFFER YOU A TERM LOAN.

ABOVE ALL, IT IS IMPERATIVE THAT I WIN MY REELECTION TO THE PRESIDENCY...

IN 1936, HE IS INVITED TO VISIT NAZI GERMANY...

THIS COUNTRY EXUDES ORDER AND A ZEST FOR LIFE. THE AIR FORCE HAS MADE INCREDIBLE PROGRESS!

*IN 1927, HE MADE A NONSTOP FLIGHT FROM NEW YORK TO PARIS.

AND ON AUGUST 1, 1936, AT THE OPENING OF THE OLYMPIC GAMES IN BERLIN...
YOU ARE A GREAT MAN, HERR HITLER! YOU'VE DONE SO MUCH FOR THE GERMAN PEOPLE.

IN 1938, LINDBERGH IS WELCOMED BY GÖRING IN BERLIN. THE HEAD OF THE LUFTWAFFE IS HIMSELF A FORMER FIGHTER PILOT...
I AM HONORED TO PRESENT YOU WITH THE CROSS OF MERIT FOR THE SERVICES YOU HAVE RENDERED TO AVIATION.

MR. LINDBERGH, WHAT DO YOU THINK OF OUR NEW AERONAUTICAL BASES?
I'M TRULY VERY IMPRESSED.

I WILL CERTAINLY INFORM MY GOVERNMENT ABOUT THE STRENGTH OF THE GERMAN AIR FORCE. WE HAVE NO INTEREST IN STARTING ANY CONFLICT WITH THE REICH!

IN OCTOBER 1940, WHEN GERMANY DEFEATED FRANCE AND MADE A PACT WITH THE USSR, LINDBERGH, IN THE UNITED STATES, SPEAKS ON THE RADIO...
OUR COUNTRY MUST RECOGNIZE THE NEW POWERS DOMINATING EUROPE!
MBS

HE MEETS HERBERT HOOVER, ROOSEVELT'S PREDECESSOR IN THE WHITE HOUSE...
MR. LINDBERGH, MY SUCCESSOR TO THE PRESIDENCY WANTS TO DRAG THE COUNTRY INTO A DANGEROUS VENTURE...
I WILL DO EVERYTHING TO KEEP US NEUTRAL!

HE ALSO MEETS HENRY FORD, THE ANTISEMITIC CAR MANUFACTURER WHO ADMIRES HITLER...
A SMALL MINORITY OF AMERICANS ARE TRYING TO GET US INVOLVED IN THE CONFLICT...
THE JEWS! THEY ARE THE ONES PUSHING US TO THE BRINK!
HOWEVER, ON NOVEMBER 5, 1940, ROOSEVELT IS REELECTED TO THE PRESIDENCY.

LINDBERGH DOESN'T GIVE UP! ON SEPTEMBER 11, 1941, DURING A MEETING IN DES MOINES THAT IS BROADCAST OVER THE AIRWAVES...
WHO ARE THE WARMONGERING AGITATORS? THE BRITISH, THE JEWS, AND THE ROOSEVELT ADMINISTRATION!
WNCA

ON THE MORNING OF DECEMBER 7, 1941, WITH SIX AIRCRAFT CARRIERS, THE JAPANESE ATTACK THE AMERICAN NAVAL BASE AT PEARL HARBOR, ON THE HAWAIIAN ISLAND OF OAHU IN THE PACIFIC OCEAN.
THE OBJECTIVE IS TO DESTROY THE UNITED STATES NAVAL POWER IN THE PACIFIC THAT IS BLOCKING ACCESS TO RESOURCES IN MALAYSIA, WHICH JAPAN ALSO ATTACKS THE SAME DAY.

THE SAME DAY, IN THE OVAL OFFICE AT THE WHITE HOUSE...

THE DAMAGE IS IMMENSE, SIR, AND NEARLY 2,500 MEN HAVE BEEN KILLED.

ON DECEMBER 11, HITLER ADDRESSES THE REICHSTAG AND DECLARES WAR ON THE UNITED STATES...

THE CREATOR HAS ENTRUSTED US WITH A HISTORICAL REVISION OF GREAT SIGNIFICANCE. IT IS NOW OUR DUTY TO ACCOMPLISH IT...

ROOSEVELT, SLOWLY BUT SURELY, IS LEADING THE WHOLE WORLD INTO WAR!

*SEE THE END OF CHAPTER 10.
** SEE CHAPTER 2.

Did Roosevelt know from American intelligence about Japan's plan to attack Pearl Harbor, and did he just let it happen? The attack did indeed allow the United States to enter the war, which the president had wanted for a long time despite opposition from the majority of the American public. There are some indications suggesting this, but no substantial evidence.

That said, why does Japan decide to challenge its powerful neighbor and "wake a sleeping giant," as a Japanese vice admiral put it? The Americans had imposed an oil embargo at the time, cutting off supplies to Japan, as the United States wanted to force Japan out of China. Before that, the Americans had stopped supplying steel to Japan.

Japanese industry and military are expanding rapidly and have few options left but to turn to the Dutch East Indies in the Pacific (modern-day Indonesia). By attacking Malaysia, Japan aims to take hold of local rubber production and target the strategic port of Singapore by crossing through Malay territory.

Note Roosevelt's masterful skill as he presents the war to the American Congress on December 8, 1941, as merely "defensive" and then waits for Germany and Italy to initiate hostilities against America.

CHAPTER

THE GREAT ALLIANCE

1941–1942

WASHINGTON AIRPORT, DECEMBER 22, 1941, LATE EVENING...

THE PRESIDENT IS WAITING FOR YOU IN HIS CAR, PRIME MINISTER.

AND SOON...

WELCOME, MR. CHURCHILL, I WISH YOU A PLEASANT STAY AT THE WHITE HOUSE.
I'VE NO DOUBT ABOUT IT, MRS. ROOSEVELT, DESPITE THE CIRCUMSTANCES...
OVER THE COURSE OF THE NEXT THREE WEEKS, THE BRITISH PRIME MINISTER AND THE AMERICAN PRESIDENT WOULD MEET ON A REGULAR BASIS.

THAT VERY EVENING...
I'D LIKE TO ASK YOU, AFTER CHRISTMAS, TO SPEAK BEFORE CONGRESS.

HMM, SO BE IT. IF NECESSARY, I SHALL. BUT LET'S TRY TO AGREE ON PRIORITIES FIRST.
ALL RIGHT!

OBVIOUSLY WE'LL HAVE TO FIGHT THE JAPANESE...
THE INTERESTS OF THE BRITISH EMPIRE IN THE PACIFIC ARE AT STAKE AS WELL.

YES, THE BIGGEST THREAT, ESPECIALLY IN AFRICA, IS STILL HITLER!

OF COURSE I AGREE! AS LONG AS HIS TROOPS ARE BOGGED DOWN IN RUSSIA, HE WON'T BE ABLE TO GIVE THE IDEA OF INVADING ENGLAND ANY SERIOUS CONSIDERATION...
SO... IT'S IMPERATIVE THAT WE HELP THE RED ARMY; THEY'LL GRADUALLY DEPLETE THE REICH AND ITS ALLIES!

I'M NOT ALL THAT FOND OF COMMUNISTS...

BUT WE'LL HAVE TO SUPPLY RUSSIA WITH AS MANY WEAPONS AND EQUIPMENT AS POSSIBLE.

ON DECEMBER 10, THE JAPANESE CAPTURE GUAM FROM THE AMERICANS NEAR THE PHILIPPINES, AND ON THE 23RD, THEY TAKE OVER WAKE ATOLL, AN AMERICAN MILITARY BASE IN OCEANIA...

*LOCATED IN OCEANIA, AUSTRALIA, A FORMER ENGLISH COLONY THAT GAINED AUTONOMY, IS STILL A MEMBER OF THE BRITISH EMPIRE AT THE TIME.

GERMAN SOLDIERS STATIONED ON THE EASTERN FRONT ARE ALSO TRYING TO CELEBRATE CHRISTMAS...

NEWS FROM HOME, FINALLY!

FROHE WEIHNACHTEN, KAMERADEN!*

*MERRY CHRISTMAS, COMRADES!

ON DECEMBER 25, AT THE WHITE HOUSE, CHURCHILL PREPARES HIS SPEECH FOR THE AMERICAN CONGRESS.

THE NEXT DAY, HE ADDRESSES THE CONGRESS. THE ROOM IS PACKED.

MEMBERS OF THE SENATE, AND MEMBERS OF THE HOUSE OF REPRESENTATIVES... HERE WE ARE TOGETHER, FACING A GROUP OF MIGHTY FOES WHO SEEK OUR RUIN.
CBS
NBC
CBS
IN THE DAYS TO COME THE BRITISH AND AMERICAN PEOPLES WILL, FOR THEIR OWN SAFETY AND FOR THE GOOD OF ALL, WALK TOGETHER IN MAJESTY, IN JUSTICE, AND IN PEACE.
HOORAY HOORAY
HOORAY
HOORAY
CBS

*THE PACT FORMING AN ALLIANCE BETWEEN GERMANY, ITALY, AND JAPAN, SIGNED IN BERLIN ON SEPTEMBER 27, 1940.

ON JANUARY 17, CHURCHILL RETURNS TO ENGLAND. ON FEBRUARY 14, THE ORDER IS GIVEN TO THE BOMBER COMMAND OF THE ROYAL AIR FORCE NOT JUST TO FOCUS ON STRATEGIC TARGETS IN GERMANY...

GENTLEMEN, WE ARE GOING TO BREAK THE GERMAN POPULATION'S MORALE BY BOMBING FACTORIES AND RESIDENTIAL AREAS!

UNDER THE COMMAND OF ARTHUR HARRIS, NICKNAMED BOMBER OR BUTCH HARRIS, GERMAN CITIES ARE BOMBARDED BY, LITERALLY, TONS OF BOMBS.

YET, UNDER ROOSEVELT'S LEADERSHIP, AMERICAN INDUSTRY IS RAMPING UP TO FULL SPEED TO MAKE UP FOR THE RELATIVE LAG IN UNITED STATES WEAPONS PRODUCTION... EVEN FORD HAS TO SHIFT GEARS!

In the alliance between Great Britain and the United States after Pearl Harbor, priorities and objectives are not necessarily the same. For Churchill, it is first a question of defending the British Isles against a German invasion, then fighting Germany and Italy–the Rome-Berlin axis–in the Middle East as well as in the Mediterranean, and lastly, resisting the Japanese attack, since the interests of the British Empire–just like those of China, the Netherlands, France, and the USSR–are also threatened by Japan in the Pacific and in Asia.

Nevertheless, the two partners agree on two essential points: both Roosevelt and Churchill believe Germany must be dealt with first–it's the "Germany First" slogan–and to this end, support must be provided to Soviet Russia through the supply of equipment.

As historian Jacques Pauwels points out, although often portrayed as a "great crusade against totalitarianism," the "Good War" that the United States would wage, particularly in Europe, is also a self-serving one. America definitely has geostrategic objectives in mind (such as gaining a foothold in Europe and other world regions) as well as economic goals (like opening new markets for American industry).

CHAPTER

MEETING AT WANNSEE

1942

ON JANUARY 20, 1942, FIFTEEN HIGH-RANKING NAZI OFFICIALS ARE INVITED TO A CONFERENCE AT A VILLA IN THE ELEGANT SUBURB OF WANNSEE, SOUTHEAST OF BERLIN. A BUFFET IS PLANNED AT THE END OF THE MEETING.

*THE NOTION THAT THERE COULD BE A "JEWISH QUESTION" IS ROOTED IN ANTISEMITISM.
**ACCORDING TO HITLER, THE JEWS—SUPPOSEDLY CONTROLLING ENGLAND, THE USA, AND RUSSIA—STARTED THE WAR, BOTH IN 1914 AND 1939.

THE MEETING AT WANNSEE IS INITIALLY SCHEDULED FOR DECEMBER 9, 1941, BUT IS EVENTUALLY MOVED TO JANUARY 20, 1942...
THE JAPANESE ATTACK ON PEARL HARBOR, THE DECLARATION OF WAR ON THE UNITED STATES, THE SOVIET COUNTERATTACKS—ALL OF THIS DELAYED US.
NOW THAT THE SITUATION SEEMS STABILIZED IN THE EAST, WE MUST URGENTLY TAKE ACTION.

ON THE MORNING OF JANUARY 20, IT IS SNOWING WHEN THE FIFTEEN REPRESENTATIVES FROM VARIOUS REICH MINISTRIES AND THE SS ARRIVE AT THE VILLA.

BEFORE THE MEETING, MEN GATHER IN SMALL GROUPS AT THE BACK OF THE VILLA...
DURING THIS SEASON, THE VIEW OF THE LAKE IS MAGNIFICENT.

WHAT WILL THE TOPIC OF DISCUSSION BE TODAY?
THE JEWISH QUESTION, I THINK...

*CENTRAL OFFICE FOR REICH SECURITY, FOUNDED BY HIMMLER.

TO FULFILL THE REICHSMARSCHALL'S WISH, WE MUST ENSURE ALL ORGANIZATIONS INVOLVED ARE WORKING IN HARMONY.
IN OTHER WORDS, COORDINATING OUR ACTIONS IS CRUCIAL TO ACHIEVE THE FINAL SOLUTION TO THE JEWISH QUESTION!
IT WILL BE THE RESPONSIBILITY OF THE REICHSFÜHRER,* UNDER MY DIRECT SUPERVISION, TO MAINTAIN CONTROL OF THE WHOLE INITIATIVE, REGARDLESS OF INDIVIDUAL TERRITORIAL RESPONSIBILITIES.
DO I NEED TO REMIND YOU OF THE ACTIONS ALREADY TAKEN AGAINST THE JEWS?
OUR GOAL WAS TO EXPEL THEM FROM VARIOUS SECTORS OF GERMAN SOCIETY, THEN FROM GERMAN SOIL.

*HIMMLER.

INITIALLY, THE ONLY OPTION WAS TO INCREASE THEIR EMIGRATION.
THIS LED, IN '39, TO THE FOUNDATION OF THE CENTRAL OFFICE FOR JEWISH EMIGRATION.

BUT WITH THE WAR GOING ON, THE POLICY OF EMIGRATION PRESENTS A NUMBER OF OBSTACLES, AND NOW, NEW OPPORTUNITIES ARE OPENING UP IN THE EAST.
THAT'S WHY THE REICHSFÜHRER SS PUT AN END TO THE EMIGRATION POLICY.

THE FÜHRER HAS AGREED TO ANOTHER SOLUTION: RELOCATE THE JEWS TO THE EAST.

HOWEVER, THIS NEW PLAN IS ONLY A TEMPORARY SOLUTION.
EVEN IF IT PROVIDES VERY USEFUL EXPERIENCE FOR THE FINAL SOLUTION TO COME.

THIS ONE CONCERNS ELEVEN MILLION JEWS. I SUGGEST A COFFEE BREAK, GENTLEMEN.

*PART OF CZECHOSLOVAKIA PLACED UNDER HEYDRICH'S ADMINISTRATION BY HITLER ON SEPTEMBER 31, 1941.
**HALF JEWS: INDIVIDUALS WHOSE ANCESTRY IS PARTIALLY JEWISH.

*ERICH NEUMANN, IN CHARGE OF THE FOUR YEAR PLAN.

Most historians agree that Hitler decides to exterminate the Jews of Europe in the fall of 1941. Perhaps he foresaw the possibility that the war could end in Germany's defeat and decided to counter this by blaming the Jews, whom he held responsible for the conflict...

Did the high-ranking officials present at Wannsee, many of them state secretaries, truly understand the fate that awaited the Jews who were to be "evacuated" to the east? The protocol prepared by Eichmann and revised by Heydrich suggests that those who did not die "naturally," exhausted by forced labor, would receive an appropriate treatment designed to prevent any "Jewish resurgence."

However, even though many Germans had already been involved in the Holocaust by Bullets (as seen in the massacre at Babi Yar in Ukraine) and in other operations, a veil of secrecy seems to envelop the affair. Historian Florent Brayard noted that even Goebbels, the Nazi Minister of Propaganda, appears to be unaware of the fate of West European Jews deported to the east before October 1943. On October 4 and 6, 1943, at Posen (Poznań, in Poland), in front of the SS and regime "elites," Himmler would openly speak of the "extermination of the Jewish people." "Now you're all aware," he said, "and you will keep this to yourselves."

CHAPTER

HITLER AIMS TO END THINGS IN THE EAST

1942

BRAZIL, PETRÓPOLIS CITY, 42 MILES FROM RIO, FEBRUARY 1942.

AS AN AUSTRIAN, A JEW, AN AUTHOR, A HUMANIST, AND A PACIFIST, I HAVE ALWAYS STOOD AT THE EXACT POINT WHERE THESE EARTHQUAKES WERE THE MOST VIOLENT.*

*STEFAN ZWEIG. *THE WORLD OF YESTERDAY*. TRANSLATED BY ANTHEA BELL.

I'M SIXTY, LOTTE'S THIRTY-FOUR, BUT SHE WANTS TO LEAVE WITH ME.

THE WORST PART FOR ME IS SEEING THE GERMAN LANGUAGE BECOME THE PROPERTY OF ADOLF HITLER, THE MAN WHO HAS BROUGHT ABOUT MORE CALAMITIES THAN ANYONE ELSE IN HISTORY.

MY BOOKS ARE BEING BURNED IN GERMANY, BUT ARE BEING PUBLISHED IN ENGLISH, FRENCH, AND PORTUGUESE!

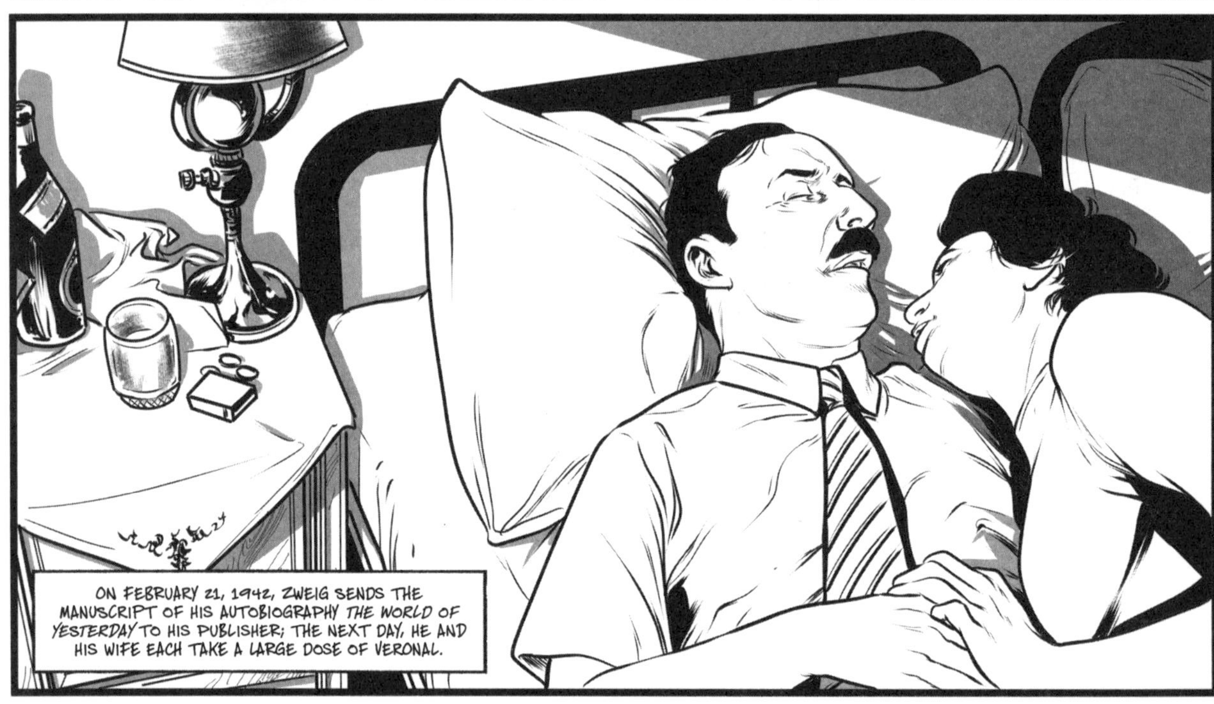
ON FEBRUARY 21, 1942, ZWEIG SENDS THE MANUSCRIPT OF HIS AUTOBIOGRAPHY *THE WORLD OF YESTERDAY* TO HIS PUBLISHER; THE NEXT DAY, HE AND HIS WIFE EACH TAKE A LARGE DOSE OF VERONAL.

*HIGH COMMAND OF THE RUSSIAN ARMY.

WHAT DO YOU THINK, COMRADES?

A DISPERSED OFFENSIVE SOUNDS RISKY, COMRADE STALIN...

THE ENEMY HAS FORTIFIED THEIR DEFENSES NEAR LENINGRAD AND IN THE SOUTHWEST. LET'S ATTACK FROM THE WEST WHERE THEY SEEM WEAKER.

COMRADE ZHUKOV, GENERAL TIMOSHENKO TOLD ME WE MUST CRUSH THE GERMANS BEFORE SPRING COMES AND THE SNOW MELTS.
END OF DISCUSSION.

STALIN IS INCREDIBLY OPTIMISTIC; SOON, HE'S PLANNING EIGHT OFFENSIVES WITH FORTY ARMIES...
WE'VE LOST THREE MILLION MEN, 20,500 TANKS, AND 21,000 PLANES, BUT WE STILL HAVE FOUR MILLION SOLDIERS!

FROM JANUARY TO MAY, THE RED ARMY FACES ONE FAILURE AFTER ANOTHER, NOTABLY AT DEMYANSK, SOUTH OF LENINGRAD, AND AT KHOLM, WHERE THE SOVIETS, EVEN AFTER HAVING THE GERMANS SURROUNDED, ARE FORCED TO RETREAT...

IN APRIL, TIMOSHENKO WANTS TO RETAKE KHARKIV IN UKRAINE, THE INDUSTRIAL FOURTH CITY OF THE USSR, A CRITICAL ROAD AND RAIL JUNCTION...

FROM MAY 12 TO 18, THE WEHRMACHT AND THE RED ARMY, COMMANDED BY TIMOSHENKO, FACE EACH OTHER HEAD-ON. BUT THE CITY REMAINS IN THE HANDS OF THE GERMANS, WHO BREAK THE RUSSIAN ENCIRCLEMENT, AND 240,000 SOVIET SOLDIERS ARE CAPTURED.

HITLER ORDERS A GRAND FUNERAL FOR THE MAN HE CALLED THE MAN WITH THE IRON HEART, ALSO KNOWN AS THE BLONDE BEAST OR THE BUTCHER OF PRAGUE. THE FÜHRER ORDERS BLOODY REPRISALS IN CZECHOSLOVAKIA.

*OPERATION BLUE.
**STILL THERE TODAY.

LENINGRAD HAS BEEN SURROUNDED SINCE SEPTEMBER 8, 1941. WHAT WAS FORMERLY SAINT PETERSBURG IS BEING DEFENDED BY SOVIET BATTERIES, AND 90,000 RESIDENTS HAVE JOINED THE RED ARMY.

THE FINNS TO THE NORTH AND THE GERMANS TO THE SOUTH HAVE BEEN STALLED FOR MANY MONTHS JUST OUTSIDE THE CITY LIMITS WHERE THE PEOPLE HAVE REFUSED TO SURRENDER.

HITLER CONSULTS WITH THE NUTRITIONIST ZIEGELMAYER.
JUST BLOCK THE CITY COMPLETELY. THE INHABITANTS WILL EVENTUALLY SURRENDER OUT OF STARVATION!

FINALLY, ON AUGUST 9, 1942, AT THE LENINGRAD PHILHARMONIC, IN THE HEART OF THE BESIEGED CITY, MUSICIANS PLAY SHOSTAKOVICH'S WORK. IT IS A MORAL VICTORY, GREETED WITH AN OVATION THAT LASTS AN HOUR.

The siege of Leningrad by the German army is one of the longest in history, and the Soviets wouldn't see their way out of it until the end of January 1944, after roughly nine hundred days. The night Shostakovich's Symphony no. 7 is performed in the city, by starving musicians, speakers broadcast the music into the streets, and even the enemy can hear it...

As for Hitler's offensive aimed at the Caucasus, the Germans manage to seize Maykop in early August 1942, but the Soviets have rendered the oil fields there unusable in the meantime. The offensive doesn't reach Grozny or Baku, and by September, Operation Fall Blau is stalled.

The idea is to clamp down on the Allies: seize the Caucasus oil in the east and capture the Suez Canal in Egypt in order to gain control of oil in the Middle East. These two sides of the clamp would then close in—maps of the Middle East had already been printed to this end by the German high command; a plan that would never come to fruition.

In June 1942, however, Rommel successfully captures Tobruk in Libya, where 35,000 to 40,000 British are taken prisoner—a terrible blow for Churchill, following the loss of Singapore, which falls into the hands of the Japanese in mid-February '42... The great writer Stefan Zweig, who took his own life on February 22, likely believed Nazi Germany would emerge victorious from the ongoing conflict.

CHAPTER

15

A CHANGE IN THE WIND

1942–1943

*REFER TO CHAPTER 11.

EARLY JUNE '42...
WE'RE GOING TO OCCUPY MIDWAY, A SMALL ATOLL WEST OF HAWAII... THAT WILL THEN ALLOW US TO TAKE HAWAII. DISMISSED!

FOUR AIRCRAFT CARRIERS OF THE IMPERIAL JAPANESE NAVY, CARRYING 256 PLANES, HEAD OUT TOWARD MIDWAY...
I'M GOING TO CREATE A DIVERSION ATTACK FAR TO THE NORTH, IN THE ALEUTIAN ISLANDS.

WHILE REALLY MY INVADING FORCES, WITH THE BATTLESHIP YAMATO, FIVE HUNDRED MEN, AND THE CARRIERS, WILL BE HEADING TO MIDWAY... AFTER THAT, WE'LL TAKE HAWAII AND DESTROY THE AMERICAN FLEET.

MEANWHILE, IN PEARL HARBOR...
ADMIRAL NIMITZ, WE'VE INTERCEPTED A JAPANESE MESSAGE AND CRACKED THEIR CODE: THEY'RE LAUNCHING AN ATTACK ON MIDWAY!
DAMN IT! WE'LL BE READY FOR THEM.

CHESTER NIMITZ, COMMANDING THE PACIFIC FLEET, RALLIES AIRCRAFT CARRIERS ENTERPRISE AND HORNET TO JOIN THE HASTILY REPAIRED YORKTOWN, UNDER REAR ADMIRAL FLETCHER.
ON JUNE 4, 1942, AT 4:30 IN THE MORNING, 108 JAPANESE PLANES ATTACK MIDWAY. THE AMERICAN FIGHTERS AND ANTIAIRCRAFT GUNS QUICKLY RESPOND, THWARTING THE ATTACK.
AT 10 A.M., AMERICAN BOMBERS LAUNCH THEIR OWN ATTACK, DECIMATING JAPANESE CRUISERS AND AIRCRAFT CARRIERS. THE EMPIRE OF THE RISING SUN IS SEVERELY HIT, MARKING A TURNING POINT IN THE PACIFIC WAR.

GENERALFELDMARSCHALL ROMMEL, LEADING THE GERMAN-ITALIAN FORCES IN AFRICA, CAPTURES TOBRUK FROM THE BRITISH ON JUNE 21, 1941. AFTER MONTHS OF GRUELING CAMPAIGNING, HE RETURNS TO GERMANY TO RECUPERATE. ON OCTOBER 24, 1942...

THE NEXT DAY, AT 5:30 P.M., ROMMEL LANDS AT QASABA, EGYPT, WHERE A FIESELER STORCH AWAITS HIM.

AT 11:25 P.M., HE REACHES HQ AND CONTACTS HIS TROOPS.

HE'LL BATTLE AGAINST GENERAL MONTGOMERY, THE NEWLY APPOINTED COMMANDER OF THE 8TH BRITISH ARMY.

MONTY IS AN OUTSTANDING ORGANIZER AND VERY POPULAR WITH HIS MEN, BUT ALSO EXTREMELY CAUTIOUS.
DESPITE CHURCHILL'S WISHES, WE WON'T ATTACK UNTIL OUR TROOPS ARE FULLY PREPARED FOR THE OFFENSIVE.

THE BRITISH HAVE 195,000 MEN COMPARED TO ROMMEL'S 105,000.
WE'RE SHORT ON SUPPLIES AND FUEL, DESPITE ALL THOSE SWEET PROMISES MADE BY THE DUCE, THE FÜHRER, AND GÖRING... BUT WE SHALL PREVAIL!

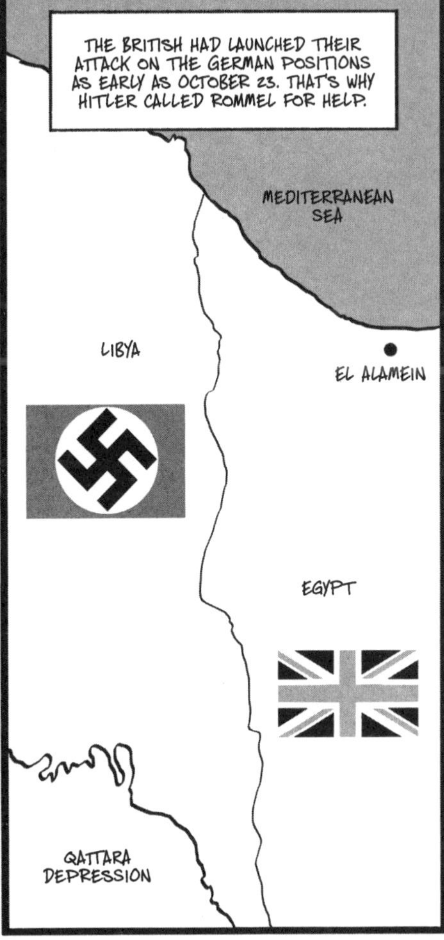
THE BRITISH HAD LAUNCHED THEIR ATTACK ON THE GERMAN POSITIONS AS EARLY AS OCTOBER 23. THAT'S WHY HITLER CALLED ROMMEL FOR HELP.
MEDITERRANEAN SEA
LIBYA
EL ALAMEIN
EGYPT
QATTARA DEPRESSION

ON OCTOBER 26, ROMMEL BRINGS THE PANZERS BACK TOGETHER TO LAUNCH A COUNTERATTACK...
BUT ON NOVEMBER 1, AN IMPROMPTU OFFENSIVE BY MONTGOMERY, CALLED "SUPERCHARGE," SHATTERS THE AXIS DEFENSES.
BY NOVEMBER 3, ROMMEL IS FORCED TO ORDER A RETREAT. THE BRITISH CAPTURE 30,000 PRISONERS. THE MYTH THAT GERMANY IS INVINCIBLE IS NOW CHALLENGED.

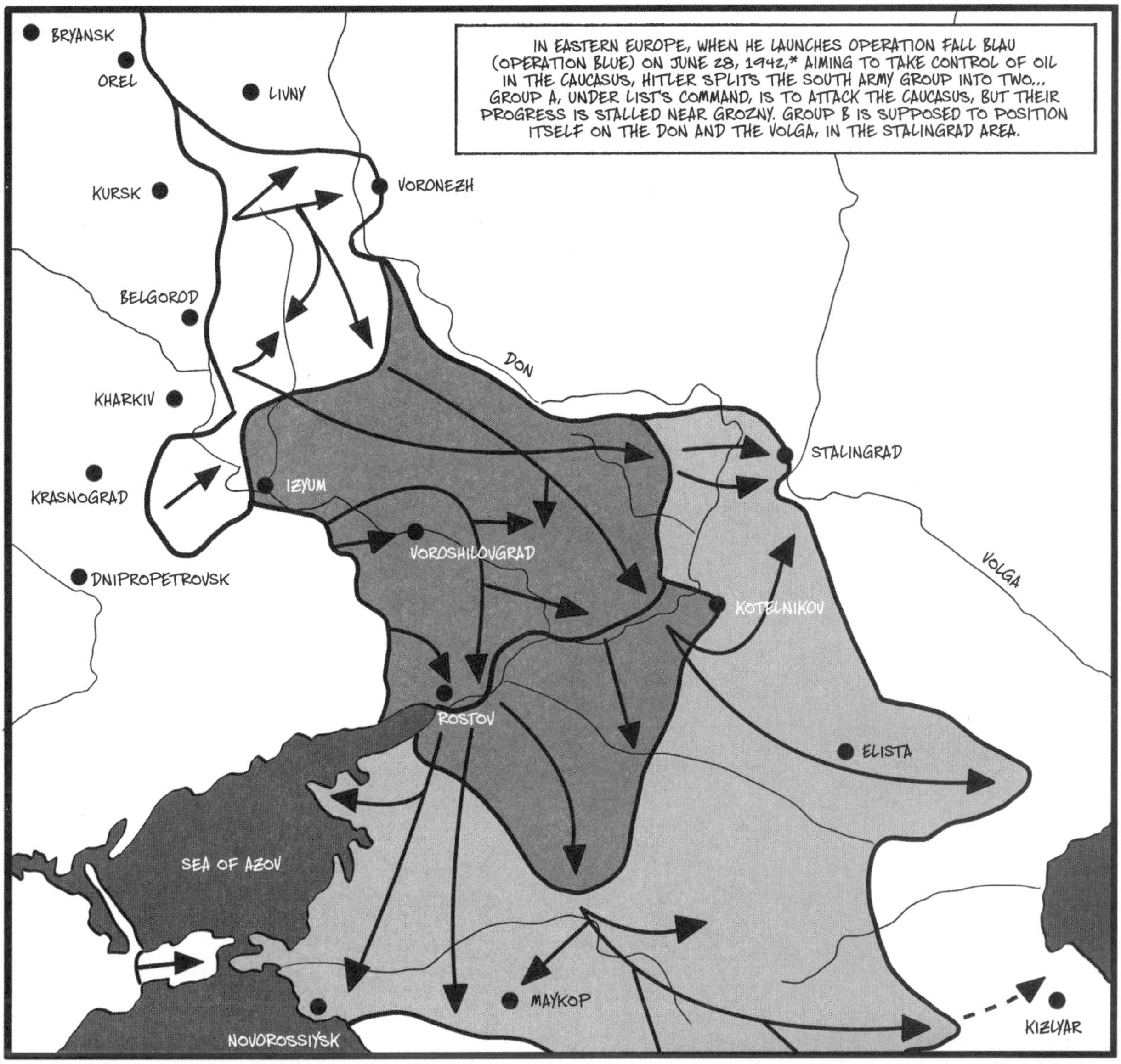

IN EASTERN EUROPE, WHEN HE LAUNCHES OPERATION FALL BLAU (OPERATION BLUE) ON JUNE 28, 1942,* AIMING TO TAKE CONTROL OF OIL IN THE CAUCASUS, HITLER SPLITS THE SOUTH ARMY GROUP INTO TWO... GROUP A, UNDER LIST'S COMMAND, IS TO ATTACK THE CAUCASUS, BUT THEIR PROGRESS IS STALLED NEAR GROZNY. GROUP B IS SUPPOSED TO POSITION ITSELF ON THE DON AND THE VOLGA, IN THE STALINGRAD AREA.

BRYANSK
OREL
LIVNY
VORONEZH
KURSK
BELGOROD
DON
KHARKIV
STALINGRAD
IZYUM
KRASNOGRAD
VOROSHILOVGRAD
VOLGA
DNIPROPETROVSK
KOTELNIKOV
ROSTOV
ELISTA
SEA OF AZOV
MAYKOP
KIZLYAR
NOVOROSSIYSK

*SEE CHAPTER 14.
**THE VOLGA, SUPPLY ROUTE FOR RUSSIAN OIL TRANSPORT.

*THE CITY IS NAMED AFTER HIM...

BUT THE NEXT DAY, ZHUKOV LAUNCHES A COUNTEROFFENSIVE WITH SIX SOVIET ARMIES, WIPING OUT THE ROMANIAN DEFENSE THAT WAS ALLIED WITH THE GERMANS...

ON NOVEMBER 23, THE RUSSIANS SUCCEED IN SURROUNDING VON PAULUS'S 6TH ARMY AND PART OF THE 4TH ARMY, TRAPPING 250,000 GERMANS.

GÖRING THEN PROMISES HITLER THAT AN AIRLIFT WILL SAVE VON PAULUS, WHILE VON MANSTEIN WILL LAUNCH AN ATTACK ON STALINGRAD.

HOWEVER, VON MANSTEIN IS PUSHED BACK BY THE SOVIETS, AND ON FEBRUARY 2, 1943, VON PAULUS AND 101,000 GERMANS SURRENDER TO THE RUSSIANS.
FALL BLAU HAS OFFICIALLY FAILED.

As historian François Kersaudy observes in his essay on Stalingrad, "on both sides of the front line, strategy is dominated by a single man, which explains the errors of the past as well as the disasters still to come." Indeed, Stalin and Hitler rely more on their instincts than on information from their intelligence services or advice from their generals...

Nevertheless, with the vastness of Russia's human reservoir–which the Soviets do not spare in the least–as well as materiel support from England and America, Germany is now on the defensive in the east as of the Battle of Stalingrad, which has marked a significant turning point.

The situation is similar in Africa, which is apparently considered a secondary theater of operations by Hitler. On November 8, 1942, Anglo-American forces land in Algeria and Morocco (Operation Torch). For Churchill and Roosevelt, this is to establish a foothold from which to eventually reconquer Europe...

As Rommel notes with great perception in his diaries: "By declaring war on the United States, we are putting the entirety of America's industrial power at the service of the allied war production."

CHAPTER

TOTAL WAR

1943

UPON THEIR ARRIVAL IN NORTH AFRICA IN NOVEMBER 1942, THE ALLIES TAKE MOROCCO AND ALGERIA (OPERATION TORCH) AGAINST RESISTANCE FROM THE VICHY REGIME. MEANWHILE, VICHY HANDS TUNISIA OVER TO THE GERMANS.
ANFA HOTEL
JANUARY 14, 1943, IN CASABLANCA, MOROCCO. ALLIED SUMMIT CONFERENCE AT THE ANFA HOTEL.

HERE WE HAVE FRENCH GENERAL GIRAUD, FAVORED BY THE AMERICAN PRESIDENT, AND THEN DE GAULLE, WHOM CHURCHILL PREFERS. STALIN IS INVITED BUT IS UNABLE TO ATTEND, HELD BACK BY EVENTS IN STALINGRAD.

WELL, GENTLEMEN, LET'S SHAKE HANDS!
RIGHT OH!

THE TWO FRENCHMEN ARE NOT INVITED TO THE DISCUSSIONS THAT ARE STRICTLY MILITARY IN NATURE...
I'VE HEARD, WINSTON, THAT YOU REMARKED AFTER OUR LANDING IN NORTH AFRICA...
"THIS IS NOT THE END. IT IS NOT EVEN THE BEGINNING OF THE END. BUT IT IS, PERHAPS, THE END OF THE BEGINNING"?

YOU ARE WELL-INFORMED, I DID SAY THAT, INDEED. I SERIOUSLY BELIEVE WE'VE TURNED A CORNER. MONTGOMERY DID WONDERS AT EL ALAMEIN.

ALL RIGHT. YOU MUST KNOW, WINSTON, OUR RUSSIAN ALLY IS URGING US TO OPEN A NEW FRONT IN EUROPE AS SOON AS POSSIBLE BECAUSE THE WEHRMACHT IS STILL HANGING ON IN THE EAST.

GERMANY FIRST; WE NEED TO DEFEAT GERMANY BEFORE WE DO ANYTHING ELSE. I AGREE WITH THAT... LET'S STRIKE THE AXIS AT ITS WEAK POINT, ITALY!

HMM, THE PACIFIC IS DEMANDING ALL MY ATTENTION. WE DEFEATED THE JAPANESE AT MIDWAY, WE'RE BUSY CRUSHING THEM AT GUADALCANAL, BUT THEY'RE NOT DOWN YET...

BUT WE COULD CONSIDER A LANDING IN SICILY TO START RELIEVING STALIN, AS SOON AS WE'VE SETTLED THE SITUATION IN TUNISIA.
ALL RIGHT. WHILE WE'RE WAITING FOR SOMETHING BETTER...

AFTER THEIR VICTORY AT MIDWAY IN JUNE 1942, THE AMERICANS GO ON THE OFFENSIVE IN THE SOLOMON ISLANDS, LOCATED IN THE SOUTH PACIFIC, WHERE THE JAPANESE OCCUPY VARIOUS BASES.
THEY LAND ON GUADALCANAL ON AUGUST 7, 1942.
AFTER CAPTURING THE ISLAND AND ITS AIRFIELD, THE AMERICANS FEND OFF RELENTLESS JAPANESE ATTACKS AS THEY ATTEMPT TO RECLAIM THE STRATEGIC BASE IN OCTOBER.
BY EARLY FEBRUARY 1943, THE JAPANESE FINALLY EVACUATE COMPLETELY. LOSSES ON BOTH SIDES ARE HEAVY, BUT AMERICAN VICTORY IS UNDENIABLE.

AT THE SAME TIME IN GERMANY, EVERYONE IS SHOCKED ON HEARING NEWS OF THE DEFEAT AT STALINGRAD. HITLER IS SILENT AND GOEBBELS, THE NAZI MINISTER OF PROPAGANDA, DECIDES TO TAKE ACTION...

*IN MAY '43.
**ARTHUR TEDDER, BRITISH AIR MARSHAL.

FINALLY, AT DAWN ON JULY 10, PARATROOPERS ARE DROPPED IN AND 2,600 SHIPS LAND EIGHT DIVISIONS IN SICILY.

THE GERMANS AND ITALIANS, CAUGHT BY SURPRISE, PUT UP A FIERCE RESISTANCE. BUT MONTGOMERY AND PATTON WOULD PREVAIL: ON AUGUST 16, MESSINA IS CAPTURED.

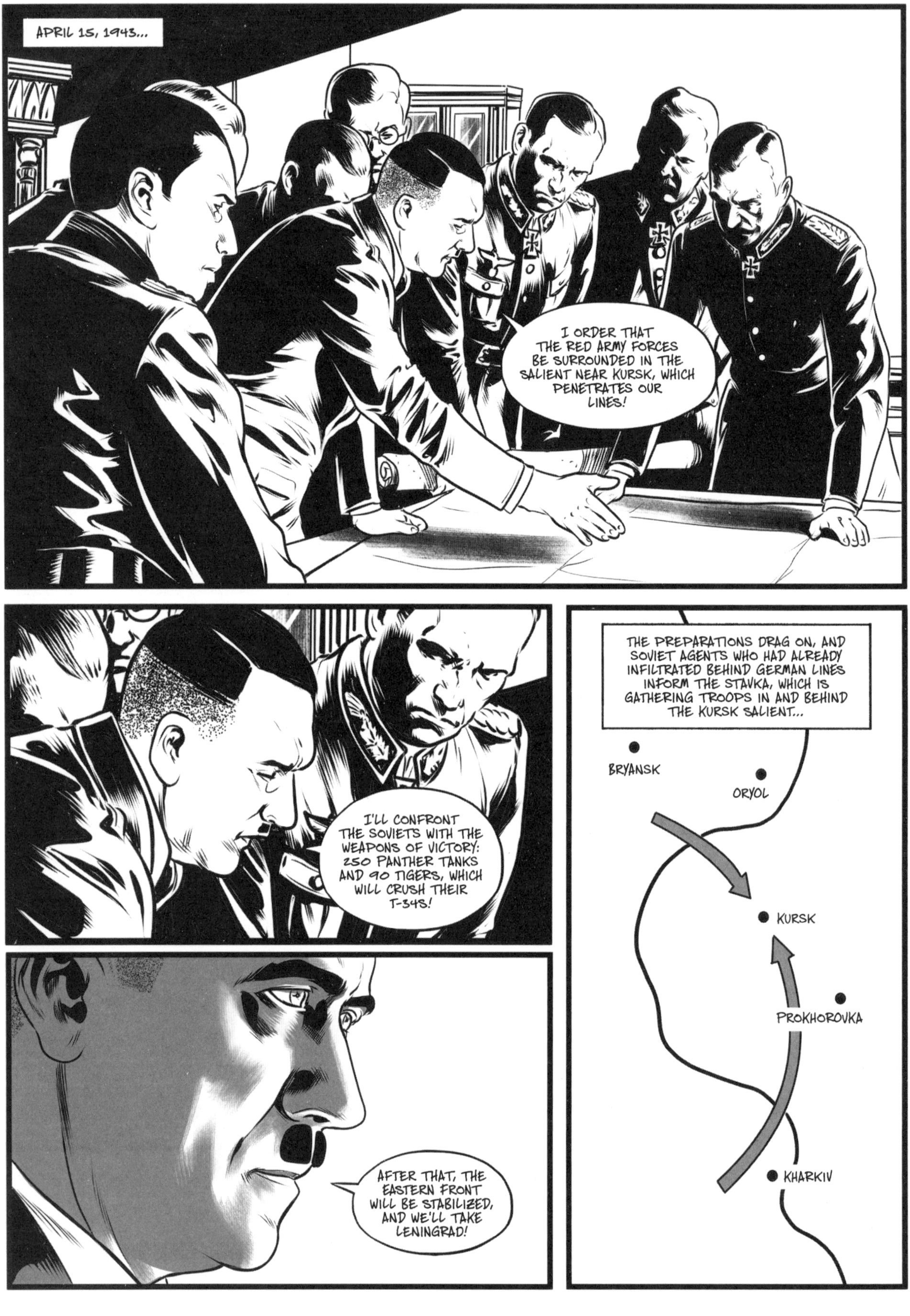

APRIL 15, 1943...

I ORDER THAT THE RED ARMY FORCES BE SURROUNDED IN THE SALIENT NEAR KURSK, WHICH PENETRATES OUR LINES!

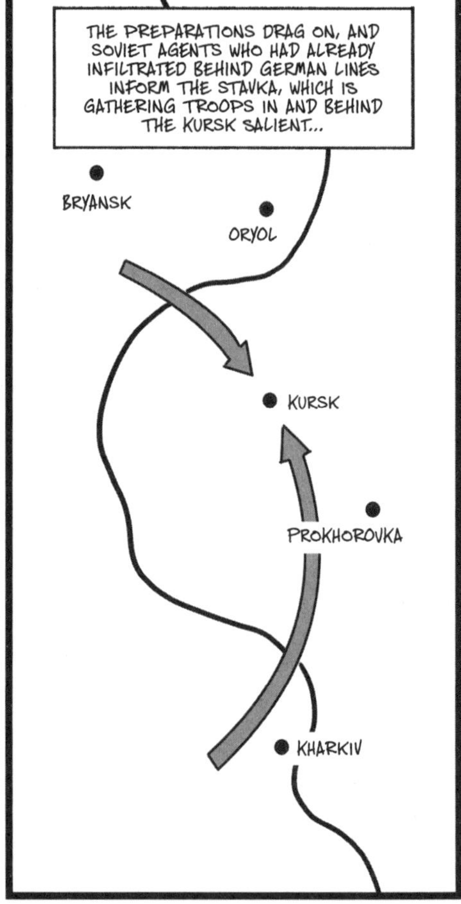

WHEN OPERATION CITADEL FINALLY STARTS ON JULY 5, THE RUSSIANS ON THE GROUND OUTNUMBER THE GERMANS. ON JULY 12, 850 SOVIET TANKS HEAD INTO COMBAT AGAINST MORE THAN 700 GERMAN ARMORED VEHICLES.
THE LARGEST TANK BATTLE IN HISTORY TURNS TO THE RED ARMY'S ADVANTAGE. THE GERMANS HAVE NOW LOST THEIR STRATEGIC INITIATIVE IN THE EAST FOR GOOD.

Kursk, perhaps even more so than Stalingrad, represents a turning point in the war in the east: from here on out, the Germans find themselves on the defensive. They lose the initiative along with their strategic reserves.

More fundamentally, Churchill would write in his memoirs after the war that the United States entering the conflict–providing materiel support to both the British and the Soviets–was a decisive moment: "we had won after all! [...]. Hitler's fate was sealed. Mussolini's fate was sealed. As for the Japanese, they would be ground to powder. All the rest was merely the proper application of overwhelming force."

It seems Hitler did actually understand that the tide was turning against him. He was even more inclined to blame the Jews, whom he held responsible for starting the conflict. On the evening of June 23, 1943, at the Berghof, he lashes out at Henriette Hoffmann, the daughter of his personal photographer and wife of Baldur von Schirach, the leader of the Hitler Youth. She dares to question him about the scenes she witnessed in the Netherlands, where Jews were being taken. He starts shouting, cupping his hands, and saying that the blood of 10,000 Germans is flowing every day and that "equilibrium" must be restored.

CHAPTER

"THEY'RE COMING!"

1943–1944

*WOLF'S LAIR.
**OTTO SKORZENY, COMMANDER OF THE 502ND SS JÄGER BATTALION.

THE DUCE MUST NOT, UNDER ANY CIRCUMSTANCES, FALL INTO THE HANDS OF THE ALLIES: I CHARGE YOU TO FIND HIM AND BRING HIM TO ME!

AS FOR ITALY... I DON'T ENTIRELY TRUST FIELD MARSHAL KESSELRING, WHO IS ON THE GROUND... I'VE ASKED GENERAL STUDENT TO INTERVENE.

YOUR MISSION IS SECRET; I'VE INFORMED STUDENT. AND HIMMLER IS AWARE, OF COURSE.

ON SEPTEMBER 7, IN ITALY...
MEIN FÜHRER, I HAVE LEARNED THAT THE AMERICAN GENERAL TAYLOR IS IN THE COUNTRY, READY TO NEGOTIATE THE ITALIAN GOVERNMENT'S SURRENDER; MUSSOLINI RISKS BEING HANDED OVER TO THE AMERICANS...

IT'S NOT TOO LATE! DID YOU MANAGE TO LOCATE THE DUCE?
JAWOHL, MEIN FÜHRER!

ON SEPTEMBER 12 AT 1:30 P.M., IN TWELVE DFS-230 GLIDERS, SKORZENY'S COMMANDOS TAKE OFF TOWARD GRAN SASSO, A SKI RESORT NORTH OF ROME.

THEY LAND NEAR THE HOTEL WHERE MUSSOLINI IS "LODGING."

AND SOON...
DUCE, THE FÜHRER HAS SENT ME TO FREE YOU...

I'M TAKING YOU TO MUNICH!

THE GERMANS ARE OCCUPYING ROME AND CENTRAL AND NORTHERN ITALY.

THEY SET UP MUSSOLINI AS THE HEAD OF A PUPPET STATE, THE ITALIAN SOCIAL REPUBLIC (RSI), IN SALÓ.

WITH GREAT DIFFICULTY, THE ALLIES CONTINUE THEIR ADVANCE THROUGH THE PENINSULA, NOW ENGULFED IN A CIVIL WAR BETWEEN PRO- AND ANTI-FASCIST GROUPS. FROM JANUARY TO MAY 1944, THE ALLIES AND THE GERMANS FIGHT AT MONTE CASSINO, THE STRONGHOLD OF THE GERMAN DEFENSE LINE.

THE ABBEY, FOUNDED IN 529, IS DESTROYED. THE ALLIES, EVENTUALLY VICTORIOUS, LOSE 105,000 MEN, WHILE THE GERMANS LOSE 80,000.

AFTER BREAKING THROUGH THE GUSTAV LINE, THE ALLIES LIBERATE ROME, WHICH SURRENDERS WITHOUT A FIGHT ON JUNE 4.

ANOTHER LANDING BEGINS ON AUGUST 15 IN PROVENCE, WITH FRENCH COMMANDOS TAKING PART...

*THEY'RE COMING!

THE OPENING OF THE NEW FRONT IN WESTERN EUROPE—PERHAPS DELAYED BY CHURCHILL, WHO IS FEELING UNEASY ABOUT THE SOVIETS ADVANCING TOO QUICKLY ON THE CONTINENT—LET THE RUSSIANS SHIFT THE SITUATION BACK TO THE EAST.
BY LATE 1943 AND EARLY 1944, THEY HAD BEGUN TO RECAPTURE, ONE BY ONE, THE POSITIONS TAKEN BY THE GERMANS AND THEIR ALLIES SINCE THE BARBAROSSA OFFENSIVE.

JULY 20, 1944, AT THE FÜHRER'S HEADQUARTERS IN EAST PRUSSIA...
WE MUST TRY BY ANY AND ALL MEANS TO PROTECT GERMANY FROM AN ALLIED OFFENSIVE, WHETHER FROM THE EAST OR THE WEST...

THE DUCE, ON THE OTHER HAND, WANTS TO TAKE BACK THE ITALIAN DIVISIONS STATIONED HERE, TO FIGHT WITH THEM AGAINST THE PARTISANS IN THE PENINSULA.
ONCE IN ITALY, THESE MEN COULD END UP DESERTING TO GO AND JOIN THEIR FAMILIES.

HMM, YES. I'M WAITING FOR MUSSOLINI, WHO IS COMING IN BY SPECIAL TRAIN. I WILL DISCUSS IT WITH HIM.

IN THE AFTERNOON...
WE'RE APPROACHING THE WOLF'S LAIR, BUT THE TRAIN HAS BEEN DIVERTED. WHAT'S GOING ON?!

*COLONEL CLAUS VON STAUFFENBERG, WHO PLANTED THE BOMB THAT JUST MISSED HITLER.

In the weeks following the failed assassination attempt on July 20, 1944, the Nazis come down hard on the plot participants, as well as anyone suspected of supporting them in any way.

Hitler, protected by the "devil's luck," has already escaped various assassination attempts. But this is the first time one was prepared within the ranks of the Wehrmacht. A brilliant officer like Rommel is himself caught in the crossfire, driven to suicide on October 14, 1944.

To many German army officers, it is becoming clear that the Führer is leading the country to disaster. Reports of Hitler's meetings with his staff show that he keeps criticizing "the army," calling it treacherous and incompetent. With regard to the Atlantic Wall, a series of bunkers built to protect the "Fortress Europe," Hitler would later say the military had only shown him the "facade."

Only the Waffen-SS, the army of political soldiers under "loyal Heinrich" (Himmler), remain unaffected by the growing paranoia that is spreading through the tight circle of leaders surrounding the now desperate dictator. As for Mussolini, aware that he is not the only one besieged by "traitors," he returns to Italy, holding out some hope for the "secret weapons" his "friend" had described to him as "terrifying." However, the V1 and V2 rockets, capable of causing significant damage to the enemy, would prove powerless in terms of changing the course of the conflict.

CHAPTER

TOWARD A NEW WORLD ORDER

1944–1945

IN THE PACIFIC, THE U.S. NAVY AND AIR FORCE NOW EXCEED JAPANESE CAPABILITIES. THE U.S. NAVY BEGINS TAKING BACK THE PHILIPPINES, WHICH WILL DESTROY A LARGE PORTION OF JAPAN'S IMPERIAL NAVY.
ON OCTOBER 20, 1944, GENERAL DOUGLAS MACARTHUR LANDS IN LEYTE GULF IN THE PHILIPPINES. BY DECEMBER 31, THE JAPANESE ABANDON THE ISLAND.

ON THE EUROPEAN CONTINENT, PARIS IS LIBERATED BY THE ALLIES ADVANCING FROM NORMANDY ON AUGUST 25, AND BRUSSELS IS FREED ON SEPTEMBER 3. THE AMERICANS GET CLOSER TO THE GERMAN CITY OF AACHEN. ON SEPTEMBER 16...
WE'RE GOING TO STRIKE IN THE ARDENNES, WHERE WE BROKE THROUGH BACK IN 1940!

JODL, CHIEF OF OPERATIONS IN THE WEHRMACHT* HIGH COMMAND, IS WORKING ON DIFFERENT PLANS IN SECRET...

EARLY OCTOBER...
MEIN FÜHRER, CROSSING THE RHINE SHOULD BE OUR PRIORITY.
THAT WILL DO PERFECTLY, JODL. CONTINUE WITH THE PREPARATIONS.

WE'LL SEND THEM THE SEVENTY-TON TIGER II TANKS!

*OKW.

HITLER ABANDONS HIS EAST PRUSSIA HEADQUARTERS, AND ON DECEMBER 2, GATHERS THE OPERATION'S LEADERS TOGETHER IN BERLIN...
FOR THE TIME BEING, WE'RE GOING TO IGNORE THE SOVIETS BECAUSE WE MUST STRIKE AT THE ANGLO-AMERICANS IF WE WANT TO ACHIEVE VICTORY. YOUR MISSION: BREAK THROUGH THE AMERICAN FRONT IN THE ARDENNES, THEN RETAKE THE PORT OF ANTWERP!

ON DECEMBER 16, AT 5:30 A.M., THE 6TH SS PANZER ARMY, COMMANDED BY SEPP DIETRICH, LAUNCHES THE OFFENSIVE, STRIKING MALMEDY, EUPEN, AND SAINT-VITH. THE 5TH PANZER ARMY, LED BY VON MANTEUFFEL, IS ALSO ON THE MOVE.

INITIALLY CAUGHT OFF GUARD, THE AMERICANS LAUNCH A COUNTEROFFENSIVE ON DECEMBER 22, UNDER PATTON'S COMMAND.

ON DECEMBER 27, THE SIEGE IS LIFTED IN BASTOGNE. MONTGOMERY, IN TURN, LAUNCHES A SUCCESSFUL COUNTERATTACK ON JANUARY 3.
IN HIS NEW YEAR'S RADIO ADDRESS IN GERMANY, HITLER REFRAINS FROM MENTIONING THE ARDENNES.

HITLER TAKES A CONSIDERABLE RISK IN DECIDING TO STRIP THE EASTERN FRONT AS PART OF HIS FINAL OFFENSIVE IN THE ARDENNES, AND THE SOVIETS SEIZE THE OPPORTUNITY. ON JANUARY 12, 1945, THEY LAUNCH A MAJOR CAMPAIGN FROM THE VISTULA.
ON JANUARY 17, IN POLAND, THEY CAPTURE WARSAW AND ENTER ŁÓDŹ ON THE 18TH. POZNAŃ IS SURROUNDED ON THE 22ND AND CAPTURED ON THE 25TH. BY EARLY FEBRUARY, THE RUSSIANS REACH THE BANKS OF THE ODER. THEY ARE NOW ONLY 43 TO 50 MILES FROM BERLIN.

A MEETING TAKES PLACE THAT MAKES HISTORY: CHURCHILL; PRESIDENT ROOSEVELT, WHO IS VERY WEAK; AND THEIR HOST, STALIN, WHO IS IN FULL HEALTH. AND, OF COURSE, THEIR RESPECTIVE DELEGATIONS.

ON THE MENU: CAVIAR AND VODKA, WHICH CHURCHILL GREATLY ENJOYS, BUT THERE ARE ALSO SOME TOUGH QUESTIONS TO RESOLVE!

THE ATMOSPHERE DURING THE WORKING MEETINGS WITH THE RESPECTIVE DELEGATIONS IS EXTREMELY FRIENDLY...
GENTLEMEN, IT'S ONLY A MATTER OF TIME BEFORE GERMANY CAPITULATES.

HOW CAN I ASSIST?

I BELIEVE IT'S TIME TO REVISIT HOW OUR MILITARY OPERATIONS ARE COORDINATED... OUR CHIEFS OF STAFF WILL SEE TO THAT.

SOON AFTER...
HOW WILL WE DEAL WITH GERMANY AFTER WE WIN?

*"FREE FRANCE," REPRESENTED BY DE GAULLE.

THE CONFERENCE CONCLUDES ON FEBRUARY 11. STALIN'S INFLUENCE AT YALTA WAS SIGNIFICANT: HE WOULD ASSUME CONTROL OF ALL EASTERN EUROPE, INCLUDING POLAND! AND HE WOULD NOT END UP KEEPING HIS PROMISE OF FREE ELECTIONS.

*THIS WOULD EVENTUALLY BE THE UNITED NATIONS (UN), FOUNDED ON OCTOBER 24, 1945.

*CURRENT ESTIMATE. NAZI PROPAGANDA CLAIMED 250,000 DEATHS.

What became known as the Yalta Conference, or Crimean Conference, held from February 4 to 11, 1945, aimed to resolve three fundamental issues: the fate of Germany, the spheres of influence of the Allies in post-war Europe, and the organization of a new League of Nations that would be more effective than the one that had been put in place before the war...

It would appear that in the course of this decisive week, Stalin bargains with Roosevelt for the USSR's participation in the war against Japan–once Germany is defeated–in exchange for the "communization" of Eastern Europe. The American liberals imagine that in the middle, or even short term, these satellite countries of Communist Russia would thrive. This is an overly optimistic view: the collapse of the USSR would not occur until late 1991. In the meantime, a "Cold War" would take place–the term is attributed to George Orwell, the author of *1984*–and would last a long time between the Eastern and Western blocs. Recent events show that this antagonism is not yet entirely resolved.

Moreover, it's possible that Britain, already resigned to a secondary role by the time the Yalta Conference takes place, hypocritically supported the idea of an independent Polish government–an idea that Stalin pretends to endorse–while understanding, in reality, that Poland, whose independence was the reason Britain and France declared war on Germany in 1939, would fall under Soviet control. In exchange, the Russians would refrain from intervening in the Mediterranean (Greece, Italy, and Spain).

CHAPTER

THE END

1945

ON APRIL 16, 1945, AT 3 A.M., TWO AND A HALF MILLION SOLDIERS FROM THE RED ARMY LAUNCH A MASSIVE OFFENSIVE...

IN BERLIN, HITLER SETS UP HIS HQ IN THE UNDERGROUND BUNKER OF THE REICH CHANCELLERY.

PLEASE MAKE NOTE OF THIS, FRAU JUNGE. IT'S THE AGENDA FOR THE EASTERN FRONT FIGHTERS.

FOR THE FIRST TIME, THE DEADLY JUDEO-BOLSHEVIK ENEMY IS LAUNCHING A MASSIVE ATTACK, IN AN ATTEMPT TO DESTROY GERMANY AND EXTERMINATE OUR PEOPLE... BUT THIS OFFENSIVE ON THE PART OF OUR ENEMIES WILL FAIL DESPITE EVERYTHING!

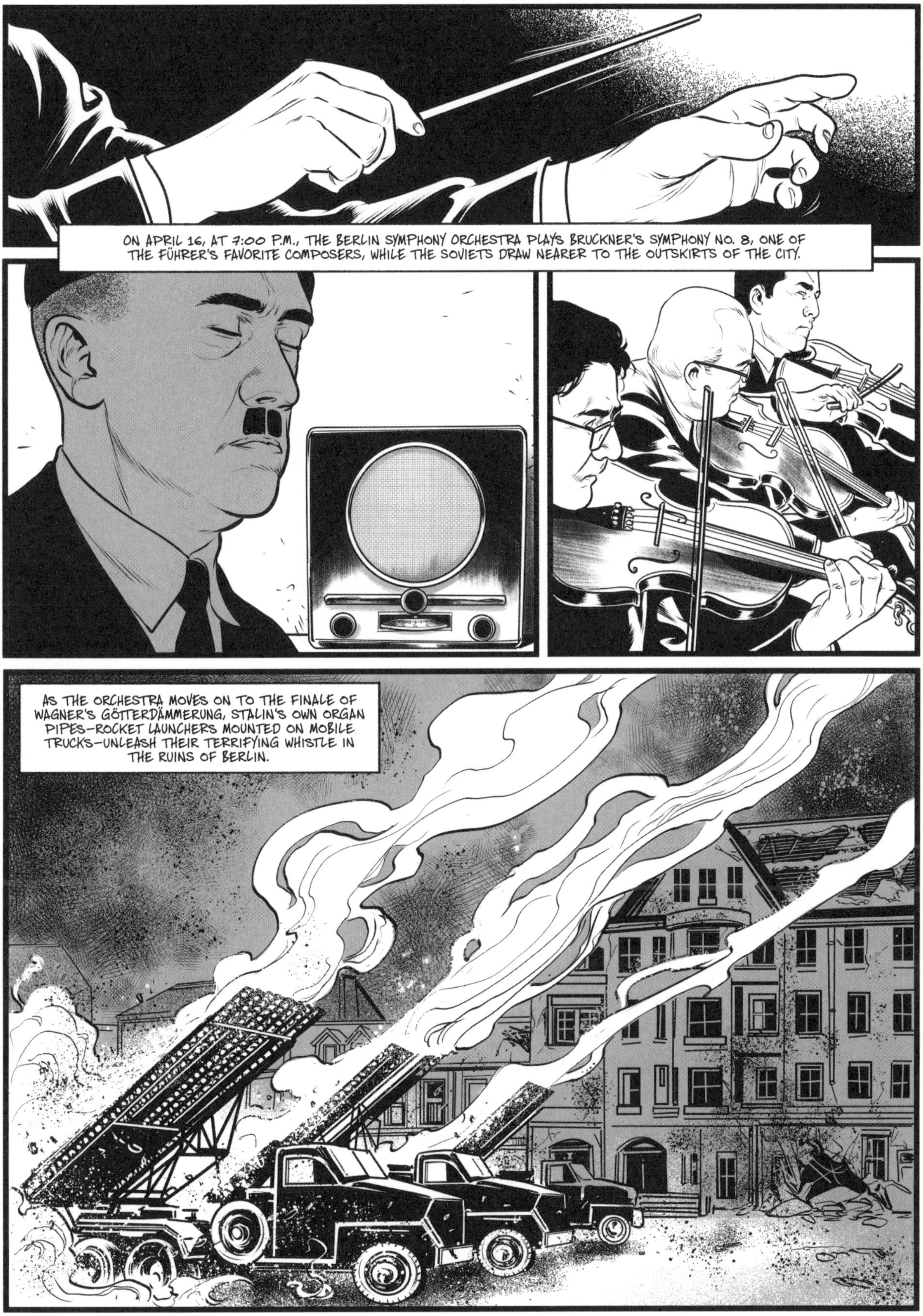

AS THE ORCHESTRA MOVES ON TO THE FINALE OF WAGNER'S GÖTTERDÄMMERUNG, STALIN'S OWN ORGAN PIPES—ROCKET LAUNCHERS MOUNTED ON MOBILE TRUCKS—UNLEASH THEIR TERRIFYING WHISTLE IN THE RUINS OF BERLIN.

ON APRIL 23, SOVIET ARTILLERY BOMBARDS THE GOVERNMENT DISTRICT.

*PEOPLE'S STORM: A MILITIA RAISED IN LATE SEPTEMBER '44 ON THE ORDERS OF BORMANN, HITLER'S SECRETARY.
**SINGLE-SHOT ANTI-TANK GRENADE LAUNCHER.

ON THE 29TH, AT PIAZZALE LORETO IN MILAN, THE BODIES OF MUSSOLINI AND HIS MISTRESS CLARA PETACCI, EXECUTED THE DAY BEFORE, ARE PUT ON DISPLAY BEFORE A VENGEFUL CROWD.

HOW HORRIFYING.

I REFUSE TO SUBMIT TO A SIMILAR FATE! I'LL ISSUE ORDERS ACCORDINGLY...

AFTER MARRYING HIS COMPANION EVA BRAUN, HITLER SHOOTS HIMSELF IN THE HEAD ON APRIL 30 AT 3:30 P.M. EVA TAKES A CYANIDE CAPSULE.

IN ACCORDANCE WITH HIS ORDERS, THEIR BODIES ARE SOAKED IN GASOLINE AND BURNED.

ON MAY 1, GOEBBELS AND HIS WIFE COMMIT SUICIDE, AFTER POISONING THEIR CHILDREN. AS NIGHT FALLS, THE OTHER OCCUPANTS OF THE BUNKER FLEE INTO BERLIN. ON MAY 2, THE RUSSIANS ENTER THE BUNKER.

ON MAY 8, GERMANY SURRENDERS UNCONDITIONALLY.

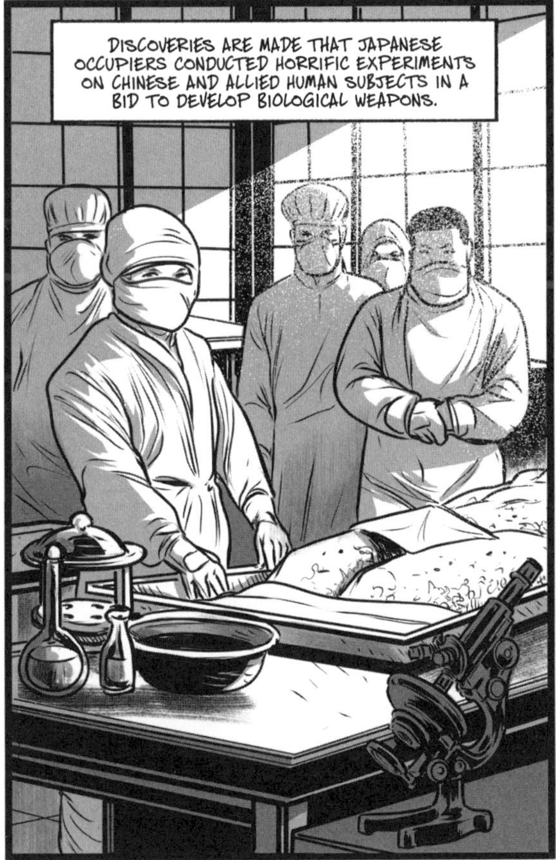

*CURRENTLY SOUGHT AFTER BY MAINLAND CHINA.

THE JAPANESE KAMIKAZE PILOTS LAUNCH THEIR PLANES LIKE BOMBS AT THE AMERICAN BATTLESHIPS, SACRIFICING THEMSELVES FOR THE HONOR OF THEIR BELEAGUERED COUNTRY...
BANZAI!

ACCORDING TO BUSHIDO, THE JAPANESE CODE OF HONOR, A WARRIOR MUST DIE RATHER THAN SURRENDER.

JULY 1945...
WE NEED TO MAKE THEM UNDERSTAND THAT WE'RE NOT GOING TO DETHRONE THEIR EMPEROR, WHOM THEY VIEW AS SACRED. OTHERWISE, THIS WILL NEVER END...

THERE IS ANOTHER POSSIBILITY: SHOCK THEM COMPLETELY BY DETONATING ATOMIC BOMBS ON THEIR TERRITORY. WE JUST HAD SUCCESS IN TESTING THEM OUT!

ON AUGUST 6 AND 9, THE CITIES OF HIROSHIMA AND NAGASAKI ARE BOMBED AND OBLITERATED.

*SEE CHAPTER 2.

Though Mussolini was executed on April 28, 1945, by the Italian resistance (more specifically, by communist partisans) and was never tried by the Allies, it isn't out of the question that the latter, who were very much present in Italy at the time, allowed this to happen… A formal trial might be difficult for London, which had long supported the Italian dictator. In this case, as in Spain—where Churchill found it preferable for Franco to remain in power after the war—the fear of the spread of communism probably explains many things.

On April 12, 1945, Roosevelt, already very weakened at the time of the Yalta Conference, passes away, while Hitler and Goebbels in the Führerbunker rejoice, hoping the Anglo-Americans will go to war against the Russians. But Vice President Harry Truman, assuming the American presidency that very day, continues the alliance with the USSR until the Reich's surrender. Only afterward will he oppose the Soviet Union during the Cold War that comes about after Germany's defeat. Moreover, it's Truman who authorizes the bombing of Hiroshima and Nagasaki.

By using the atomic bomb, developed under the direction of physicist J. Robert Oppenheimer, the United States shows everyone that they now have an absolute weapon. Russia, however, in part through espionage, also develops its own bomb by 1949. A balance of terror is thus established between the two blocs. This bipolar world would become multipolar when the Eastern Bloc finally collapses in 1991.

CHAPTER

THE TRIAL

1945–1946

HIMMLER FALLS INTO THE HANDS OF THE BRITISH AND COMMITS SUICIDE ON MAY 23, 1945. EICHMANN AND MANY OTHER NAZI OFFICIALS MANAGE TO ESCAPE. THE ALLIES, HOWEVER, CAPTURE TWENTY-ONE HIGH-RANKING MEMBERS OF THE REGIME ONE BY ONE, AND AFTER INITIALLY CONSIDERING THE POSSIBILITY OF SUMMARILY EXECUTING THEM, THEY MAKE PREPARATIONS TO BRING THEM TO JUSTICE.
THE TRIAL, SET TO BEGIN ON NOVEMBER 20 IN THE RUINS OF NUREMBERG, MARKS A WORLD FIRST.

THE COURTHOUSE IS HASTILY SET UP IN THE HEART OF THE CITY WHERE THE NAZIS USED TO GATHER. IT STILL STANDS THERE TO THIS DAY.

THE DEFENDANTS' BOX, FLANKED BY LAWYERS AND GUARDS, STANDS OPPOSITE THE AMERICAN, BRITISH, RUSSIAN, AND FRENCH MAGISTRATES...
THE MOST SIGNIFICANT AMONG THE DEFENDANTS IS HERMANN GÖRING, AN EARLY NAZI MEMBER, CLOSE ADVISOR TO THE FÜHRER, AND HEAD OF THE LUFTWAFFE AIR FORCE.
THE AMERICANS WEANED HIM OFF HIS MORPHINE ADDICTION, AND HE HAS DECIDED TO DEFEND THE DEFEATED REGIME.

*HE WAS, IN FACT, INFORMED.
**SEE CHAPTER 4.

THE SOVIET JUDGE INTERVENES...

PROSECUTOR JACKSON, WE ARE HERE TO JUDGE ONLY THOSE ACTIONS COMMITTED BY THE THIRD REICH!

OBJECTION SUSTAINED; I FORBID ANY MENTION OF THESE CLAUSES DURING THIS TRIAL, DR. SEIDL!

*SEE CHAPTER 3.

ANOTHER CHARGE: CRIMES AGAINST PEACE!

QUESTIONING OF RIBBENTROP, THE REICH'S MINISTER OF FOREIGN AFFAIRS, WOULD NEVERTHELESS DEMONSTRATE THAT, IF THE INVASION OF POLAND IN SEPTEMBER 1939 CONSTITUTES A CRIME, THEN THE SOVIET UNION SHOULD BE CONSIDERED AN ACCOMPLICE TO IT.

THIRD CHARGE: GERMANY COMMITTED WAR CRIMES! YOU TERRORIZED POLAND, YOU RAZED WARSAW—TO MENTION ONLY A FEW EXAMPLES...

FINALLY, THE FOURTH CHARGE, THE MOST SERIOUS... YOU COMMITTED A CRIME AGAINST HUMANITY, THE GENOCIDE OF THE JEWS OF EUROPE! WE ARE GOING TO SHOW YOU FOOTAGE TAKEN IN THE CAMPS WHEN THEY WERE LIBERATED.

IT'S JUST PROPAGANDA!

DURING THE SUBSEQUENT INTERROGATION...
I'M CONVINCED THE FÜHRER WASN'T AWARE OF THE DETAILS AND THE ATROCITIES COMMITTED IN THE CAMPS!

OTHER DEFENDANTS ARE STUNNED...
IT'S INDEFENSIBLE!
WE DIDN'T KNOW...

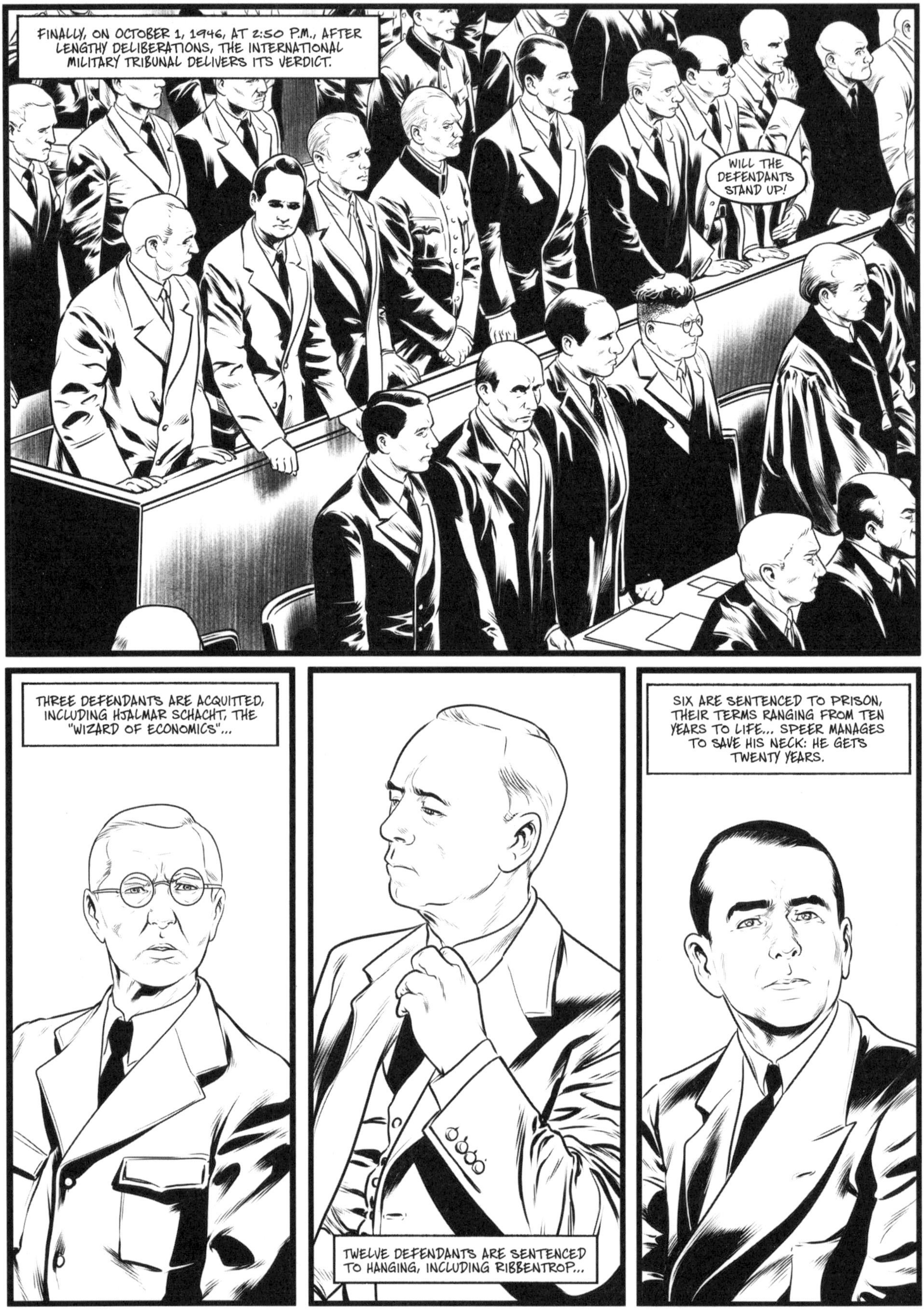

FINALLY, ON OCTOBER 1, 1946, AT 2:50 P.M., AFTER LENGTHY DELIBERATIONS, THE INTERNATIONAL MILITARY TRIBUNAL DELIVERS ITS VERDICT.

WILL THE DEFENDANTS STAND UP!

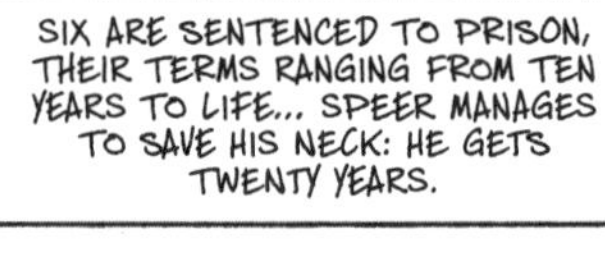

GÖRING, WITH THE HELP OF AN AMERICAN GUARD, MANAGES TO PROCURE SOME POISON...
I'M SICK, HERBERT, AND I NEED MEDICINE... I'LL TELL YOU WHERE TO FIND IT.
BITING INTO A CYANIDE CAPSULE, THE REICHSMARSCHALL ESCAPES THE HORROR OF THE GALLOWS.
ON JULY 19, 1947, THE DOORS OF SPANDAU PRISON IN WEST BERLIN CLOSE ON SIX NAZI DIGNITARIES.
ON AUGUST 17, 1987, RUDOLF HESS, WHO HAD BEEN ALONE IN SPANDAU SINCE 1966, TAKES HIS OWN LIFE AT THE AGE OF 93.

As various historians have noted, the extermination of the Jews in Europe only became a real "issue" at Nuremberg, when the Allies sought to morally condemn a defeated enemy. Prior to that, the fate of the Jews did not seem to be a chief concern for the military leaders fighting the Third Reich.

Is the trial an exercise in "victor's justice"? It was understood from the outset that only the leaders of Nazi Germany and their organizations would face judgment. Any potential war crimes committed by the Allies–such as the Katyn massacre, the bombing of Dresden, or the use of nuclear weapons on Hiroshima and Nagasaki–could not be questioned, nor could Russia's complicity with Germany in the prearranged dismemberment of Poland. The Holocaust remains a "crime against humanity" unique in its enormity and "industrial" organization, even though other genocides have occurred both before and after.

While the actions of the International Military Tribunal are, in some ways, biased and partial, they nonetheless represent a historical advancement: henceforth, war crimes or "crimes against humanity" would not go unpunished, at least in theory. In 2002, the adoption of the Rome Statute would allow for the creation of the International Criminal Court (ICC), based in The Hague. This body is a legacy of Nuremberg, even though it is not recognized by the USA, Russia, China, or Israel.

IN CONCLUSION

Dwight D. Eisenhower, the supreme commander of the Anglo-American Allied forces in Europe, stated in his memoirs in 1948: "This war has made the United States and Russia the two most powerful nations in the world [...]. Neither country was responsible for having built a colonial empire by force [...]. Ideologically, however, they were diametrically opposed..." The reference to colonial empires is important: after 1945, "old Europe" would lose its colonies, which would engage in fierce struggles for independence.

From here on out, the USA and the USSR would share the spheres of influence on a global scale. However, this new world order, inherited from a war that resulted in sixty to seventy million deaths, has since undergone three major changes:

> The gradual construction of the European Union, the third largest economic power in the world after America and China. A fragile entity, as seen with Brexit in 2020, and still anchored to the United States from a military perspective.
>
> The collapse of the USSR during the years 1989–1991, an event that inspires nostalgia for the past and resentment among current Russian leaders. The war in Ukraine that began in 2022 stemmed from this.
>
> Finally, the reawakening of China, a millennia-old empire that is once again emerging as a major power and the only one, at the beginning of the twenty-first century, capable of competing with the American superpower.

In an era where the Anthropocene—our current period in history when human impact threatens the planet—poses severe challenges, will the great nations be able to curb their tendency to resort to weapons and the massacre of entire populations in support of their expansionist ambitions? Only the future will tell.

FURTHER
READING

BIBLIOGRAPHY

General Works

Kershaw, Ian. *Choix fatidiques. Dix décisions qui ont changé le monde, 1940–1941* [*Fateful Choices. Ten Decisions That Changed the World, 1940–1941*]. Seuil, 2009.

Wieviorka, Olivier. *Histoire totale de la Seconde Guerre mondiale* [*Total History of the Second World War*]. Perrin/Ministère des Armées, 2023.

Beevor, Antony. *La Seconde Guerre mondiale* [*The Second World War*]. Calmann-Lévy, 2012.

Mongin, Dominique (ed.). *Les cinquante discours qui ont marqué la Seconde Guerre mondiale* [*The Fifty Speeches That Impacted the Second World War*]. André Versaille, 2010.

Lopez, Jean, and Olivier Wieviorka (ed.). *Les mythes de la Seconde Guerre mondiale* [*The Myths of the Second World War*]. 2 vols. Perrin, 2015 and 2017.

Hitler

Speer, *Albert. Au cœur du Troisième Reich* [*Inside the Third Reich*]. Fayard, 1971.

Trevor-Roper, H. R. *Hitler: directives de guerre* [*Hitler: War Directives*]. Arthaud, 1965.

Hitler parle à ses généraux [*Hitler Speaks to His Generals*]. Albin Michel, 1964.

Delpla, François. *Une histoire du Troisième Reich* [*A History of the Third Reich*]. Perrin, 2014.

Mussolini

Milza, Pierre. *Conversations Hitler-Mussolini*. Fayard, 2013.

Serra, Maurizio. *Le mystère Mussolini* [*The Mussolini Mystery*]. Perrin, 2021.

Milza, Pierre. *Mussolini*. Fayard, 1999.

Diplomacy

Carley, Michael J. *1939: l'alliance de la dernière chance* [*1939: The Alliance of Last Resort*]. Presses de l'Université de Montréal, 2001.

von Ribbentrop, Joachim. *De Londres à Moscou* [*From London to Moscow*]. Grasset, 1954.

Hillgruber, Andreas. *Les entretiens secrets de Hitler* [*Hitler's Secret Conversations*]. Fayard, 1969.

Schmidt, Paul-Otto. *Sur la scène internationale avec Hitler* [*On the International Scene with Hitler*]. Perrin, 2014.

Japan

Bernard, Nicolas. *La Guerre du Pacifique* [*The Pacific War*]. 2 vols., Tallandier, Texto, 2019.

Hersey, John. *Hiroshima*. Tallandier, Texto, 2011.

Birolli, Bruno. *Ishiwara: l'homme qui déclencha la guerre* [*Ishiwara: The Man Who Triggered the War*]. Armand Colin, 2012.

Great Britain

Bourneuf, Pierre-Étienne. *Bombarder l'Allemagne* [*Bombing Germany*]. PUF, 2014.

Churchill, Winston. *La Deuxième Guerre mondiale* [*The Second World War*]. 12 vols. Plon, 1948–1954.

France

Pétain, Philippe. *Appels aux Français. 1940* [*Appeals to the French. 1940*]. Plon, 1941.

de Gaulle, Charles. *Mémoires de guerre. L'Appel.* 1940–1942 [*War Memoirs. The Appeal. 1940–1942*]. Plon, 1965.

Lormier, Dominique. *Mers el-Kébir. Juillet 1940* [*Mers-el-Kébir. July 1940*]. Calmann-Lévy, 2007.

USSR

Lopez, Jean, and Lasha Otkhmezuri. *Barbarossa*. Passés Composés, 2019.

Richardot, Philippe. *Hitler face à Staline* [*Hitler versus Stalin*]. Belin, 2013.

Lopez, Jean, and Lasha Otkhmezuri. *Joukov* [*Zhukov*]. Perrin, Tempus, 2020.

Zaslavsky, Victor. *Le massacre de Katyn* [*The Katyn Massacre*]. Perrin, Tempus, 2007.

Kersaudy, François. *Stalingrad*. 2nd revised edition. Perrin, 2023.

United States

Blin, Arnaud. *Comment Roosevelt fit entrer les États-Unis dans la guerre* [*How Roosevelt Led the United States into the War*]. André Versaille, 2011.

Pauwels, Jacques. *Le mythe de la bonne guerre* [*The Myth of the Good War*]. Aden Belgique, 2005.

The Holocaust

Brayard, Florent. *Auschwitz, enquête sur un complot nazi* [*Auschwitz, Investigation into a Nazi Conspiracy*]. Seuil, 2012.

Roseman, Mark. *Ordre du jour: génocide. Le 20 Janvier 1942* [*Order of the Day: Genocide. January 20, 1942*]. Audibert, 2002.

Snyder, Timothy. *Terre noire. L'Holocauste, et pourquoi il peut se répéter* [*Black Earth. The Holocaust, and Why It Can Happen Again*]. Gallimard, 2016.

The Normandy Landings

Eisenhower, Dwight D. *Croisade en Europe* [*Crusade in Europe*]. Laffont, 1949, reissued Nouveau Monde, 2023.

Beevor, Antony. *D-Day et la Bataille de Normandie* [*D-Day and the Battle of Normandy*]. Calmann-Lévy, 2009.

The Battle of the Ardennes

Beevor, Antony. *Ardennes 1944* [*Ardennes 1944*]. Calmann-Lévy, 2015.

Bernard, Henri, and Roger Gheysens. *La Bataille d'Ardenne* [*The Battle of Ardenne*]. Duculot, 1990.

The End

Junge, Traudl. *Dans la tanière du loup* [*In the Wolf's Lair*]. JC Lattès, 2005.

Fest, Joachim. *Les derniers jours d'Hitler* [*The Last Days of Hitler*]. Perrin, 2003.

The Nuremberg Trials

David, Éric. *Nuremberg*. Racine, 2022.

Varaut, Jean-Marc. *Le Procès de Nuremberg* [*The Nuremberg Trial*]. Perrin, 1992.

Editor: Joseph Montagne
Designer: Josh Johnson
Design Manager: Pam Notarantonio
Managing Editor: Josh Weiss
Production Manager: Alison Gervais

Adapted into English by Nube Consulting
Translators: Amanda Axsom and Peter Law
Letterer: Yasmín

Library of Congress Control Number: 2025931138

HC ISBN 978-1-4197-8449-1
eISBN 979-8-88707-872-4

Printed and bound in Malaysia
10 9 8 7 6 5 4 3 2 1

ABRAMS The Art of Books
195 Broadway, New York, NY 10007
abramsbooks.com

ABRAMS is represented in the UK and Europe by Abrams & Chronicle Books, 1 West Smithfield, London EC1A 9JU and Média-Participations, 57 rue Gaston Tessier, 75166 Paris, France.
abramsandchronicle.co.uk and media-participations.com info@abramsandchronicle.co.uk